MORE THAN TRUE

MORE THAN TRUE

THE WISDOM OF
FAIRY TALES

ROBERT BLY

HENRY HOLT AND COMPANY
NEW YORK

Henry Holt and Company

Publishers since 1866
175 Fifth Avenue
New York, New York 10010
www.henryholt.com

Henry Holt ® and 🖬® are registered trademarks of Macmillan
Publishing Group, LLC.

The pictures for *More Than True* are adaptations of vintage illustrations
of the six stories included in this book (and, in the case of "One-Two Man,"
related tales, due to the scarcity of such depictions). The artists who have
been remixed into these new images include Anne Anderson, H.J. Ford,
Fred Kabotie, Theodor Kittelsen, Kay Nielsen, Gustaf Tenggren,
Otto Ubbelohde, and Hermann Vogel.

Library of Congress Cataloging-in-Publication Data

Names: Bly, Robert, author.
Title: More than true: the wisdom of fairy tales / Robert Bly.
Other titles: Wisdom of fairy tales
Description: First edition. | New York : Henry Holt and Company, 2018. |
 Includes bibliographical references and index.
Identifiers: LCCN 2017024789 | ISBN 9781250158192 (hardcover :
 alk. paper) | ISBN 9781250158208 (electronic book)
Subjects: LCSH: Fairy tales—History and criticism. | Tales—History and
 criticism. | Wisdom in literature. | Truth in literature. | Conduct of life
 in literature. | Fairy tales—Psychological aspects.
Classification: LCC PN3437 .B59 2018 | DDC 398.2—dc23
LC record available at https://lccn.loc.gov/2017024789

Our books may be purchased in bulk for promotional, educational, or
business use. Please contact your local bookseller or the Macmillan
Corporate and Premium Sales Department at (800) 221-7945, extension
5442, or by e-mail at MacmillanSpecialMarkets@macmillan.com.

First Edition 2018

Designed by Meryl Sussman Levavi

Printed in the United States of America

1 3 5 7 9 10 8 6 4 2

For my beloved wife, Ruth,
who taught me much about fairy stories

CONTENTS

INTRODUCTION

THE WISDOM OF THE ANCIENTS HINTS THAT THE OLD people know more than we do: the amazing harmonies of wedding rings imagined as gold crowns; the castles where the fat King lives; the agony of the daughter who keeps near her father by asking riddles; the great hammock let down from the stars, lovers playing on its fringes—such abundance is dazzling. The human soul arrives as a frog, having regressed since the Council of Nicaea. A boy needs the help of so many others to overcome his father's jealousy; he's subtly moved to a meadow bordering a lake, where a dragon eats sheep every night at dusk. There are stories with naked narratives that some speculate are remnants of vast festivals of narrative operas, retold in the simplest language seven hundred years later.

In Norwegian fairy tales, the storyteller kept his audience in thrall with certain possibilities of fabulous healing—changing the King to the local rich farmer, the gold services to a silver spoon, the castles to a well-built Norwegian farmhouse with towers dazzling only by comparison with the surrounding fine woods.

Other stories come down from the mystery initiations, and teachings later destroyed by forces that preferred Christianity, and were unlike ancient mass festivals in that they contained secret symbols and paid attention to stages of human growth. Some stories contain information meant for men and women on private journeys, seeking their way. And there are accounts of practices in which the community would drum around the shaman as he or she ascended, calling out from each successive "world."

Sometimes fairy tales are stories of incidents, supernatural or otherwise, told and retold, in which the psyche is trying to communicate what it knows, trying to slip something past the guards of the dictator ego, embroidering it, adding elements, altering original effects, until it finally reveals some complicated truth that the fundamental imagination has wanted to see embodied for a long time.

So the psychological genius, who might have been an observant shaman or rebel priest or wise woman of the tribe, not only had to convey some important idea—for example, the stages in development of the psyche—but also had the problem of making the stages clear, while creating incidents so vivid, so astounding, so colorful, so amusing, so obscene, so satisfying to the rebellious mind, that these incidents would not be forgotten. They hoped that the story might be remembered for hundreds or thousands of years and the details would still arrive fresh in the resonating soul ready to take them in.

Somehow, the old King and the golden-haired Princesses and the dangerous high-crested dragons with evil tempers have resonated for centuries in the unconscious mind. These Princesses and dragons are folded buds that, after several thousand years of development in language, have begun to unfold in the conscious mind, and this book is an attempt to help with the later opening, so that the conscious mind may receive the fragrance of the old stories, tales told centuries ago by male and female geniuses.

My wife, Ruth, and I have enjoyed reading and talking about fairy stories together for years. They are gifts that help both of us understand the craziness of our lives. When I decided to do this book, I realized that my job would be to use my intuition and write about stages of men's growth as I see them in these tales. I have no authority for my interpretation of themes in such stories, but I admire some astonishing thinkers on those matters: James Hillman, Ernest Becker, Gurdjieff, Ortega y Gasset, Kierkegaard, Yeats, and of course the two men who first turned over the closed box of male growth by standing on their heads and so putting their heads down near Hades. I mean those two old clowns, Freud and Jung. And now we also have the work of Martín Prechtel, Robert Moore, Robert Johnson, and Malidoma Somé.

What has endured through human history are the stories. They are amazing trees of sound that grow inside the human memory and are fed by some longing for intimacy with others. The stories examined here are fed by the praise of the group after the last word of the story is spoken. These stories are full of information; they belong to us all.

—ROBERT BLY

MORE THAN TRUE

ONE

THE SIX SWANS

As the story begins, a King, who has hunted "too hotly," is separated from the rest of the hunting party and soon finds himself lost in the forest, where he comes upon an old witch. He asks her whether she can help him find his way out of the forest. "Oh yes, indeed I can. But there's a condition first. If you don't agree to it, you won't find your way out at all and you'll starve and die here." "What's the condition then?" "Make my daughter your Queen. If you agree to that, I will help you."

The King agreed and followed the witch to her hut,

where the daughter was waiting. She was beautiful—though he did not like her. Still, he set her up on his horse and they made their way to the palace, where they soon married.

The King and his first wife had brought to birth seven children—six boys and a girl. They loved them all beyond telling. The mother had died, and since the King feared the new Queen might not treat them kindly, he kept the children so concealed in the forest that he himself could find them only by means of a ball of yarn a wise woman had given him. As the ball unrolled in front of him, he had only to follow the yarn to find the lonely castle where they lived. He went so often to see them that the new Queen grew suspicious. She commanded the servants to follow him and report back to her. They told her about the ball of yarn.

The new Queen had a plan: she made seven shirts of white silk and sewed a charm into each one. Then she found where the King had hidden the ball of yarn, took it, and followed it to the castle where the children waited for a visit from their father. When the boys ran out to greet him, the stepmother threw a shirt over each one and their bodies were changed into those of swans.

The Queen didn't know about their sister. She thought she had done away with all the children.

When the King visited the castle, he found the little girl alone and he asked about her brothers. She said they had flown over the forest in the shape of swans and now she was by herself in the castle. The King wanted to take her home with him, but the girl was afraid of the stepmother and begged him to let her stay another night. That night she walked out into the forest and kept walking day and night until she found a little hut with six beds in it. Not daring to sleep in one of the beds, she lay down on the floor, where she slept until she heard the rustle of wings and saw swans coming in through the windows. As soon as they took off their swans' skins she saw they were her brothers. They greeted each other with great joy, but soon the brothers said, "You can't stay here. Robbers live here. If they come home they'll kill you." "You can't help me?" "No. We have only a quarter of an hour as humans. Then we're swans again." The little girl said, "Can't I set you free?" "Well, if you're willing to go for six years without speaking a single word, or laughing, and to spend the whole time sewing shirts of starwort for each one of us you could—but that's too hard." Then the brothers changed to swans and flew away.

The girl left the hut and went to the forest to sit all night in a tree. When she woke she began sewing the first starwort shirt. The King of a different country was out hunting, and when his men asked her what she was doing alone in the forest, she simply kept on sewing. They kept pestering her until she threw down her jewels one by one and bits of her clothing until she was there in nothing but her slip. The men climbed the tree and brought her down for the King to question her. But she wouldn't answer.

The girl was so beautiful that the King fell in love with her. He put his mantle around her shoulders, set her on his horse, and when he got her to his castle he dressed her so richly that she shone more brightly than his palace or any of his courtiers. The King decided he must marry her, and so he did.

Meanwhile the King's mother saw that the new Queen was mute and thought she wasn't worthy of her son, so when their first child was born she took it away and smeared the mother's mouth with blood. She wouldn't speak a word in her own defense, but the King refused to think ill of her. Still, when the same thing happened two more times, the King gave his wife over to the court and she was sentenced to die by fire.

The day she was to die was the last day of the six years that she was forbidden to speak or laugh. She had finished all but the sleeve of the last shirt and she carried all six over her arm to the stake on the hill where she was to meet her death. She looked up and saw six swans flying so close to her that she was able to throw a shirt over each one. The brothers returned to their human form, except for the youngest, who still had a wing descending from his shoulder. They all kissed one another and the girl went to her husband and said, "Dear one, I have been accused, but I am innocent." And then she told him that his own mother had taken away their children and had accused her falsely. The King had great joy when he saw his wife's six brothers. He ordered his mother bound to the stake, where she was burned to death. Then the King and the Queen and the six brothers lived in peace and happiness the rest of their lives.

* * *

In the ancient tales we receive as fairy stories, a human being may suffer transformation and de-evolution: through ill luck a man or a woman may be turned into a frog as in "The Frog Prince," or into a raven or a mouse, fish, ox, and so on. A bird is another favorite. Birds inhabit both air and earth worlds. In a bird we touch on the qualities of lightness, heavenliness, freedom from earth, flight from enclosure, and ascension into light. With the swan, we have joined the water world as well.

If we consider the characters of "The Six Swans" as making up a human family, or even a single human being, we see the tangled history of the swan boy. He will eat, work, sleep, and act in earthly ways, but without the help of a father. He will have fear of conventional relationships, fear of taking one job, one career, one artistic form, or one religion. He is full of longing, and he can fly long distances and migrate to other countries. He prefers light to dark and the transpersonal to the person. He feels himself to be special. Even when he becomes a man in body, his psyche will remain "the eternal boy" or the *"puer aeternus."* He senses something precious and secret inside himself, and he is aware that a relationship might destroy that precious thing. He becomes a "boy god." For a young male with such longings, fears, and abilities, a bird does very well as a symbol—and the long-necked swan even better.

I feel something immensely significant in the brief scene of the King's turning to a negative female power for help in leaving the forest. The King has been hunting too hotly and is lost. How much do we know of the early life of our fathers? This introductory drumroll to the story seems a true prelude for the lives of so many men I know. The King chooses protection from the risk of finding his own way and chooses magical escape over discipline and suffering. With that rejection of risk, he rejects his own destiny. This is a common choice in a culture such as ours in which the help that would have come through initiation has been lost.

Adults live in fear of one kind or another—fear of failure, poverty, isolation, fear of loss of soul in the destruction of the earth. Those fears create a mood of "being lost in the forest." Men in their twenties and thirties respond to those fears by leaning on a corporation, or an addiction, and sometimes by living off a woman, which can have the unanticipated effect of putting him in touch with a negative side of her nature.

The King's solution, when fearing for his own life, was to accept the witch's way out.

After his children are hidden away in the forest, the King is in a relatively comfortable situation, and he dozes away and dreams of what actually needs to be done— while his Queen makes de-evolving shirts for his off-spring. In fairy tales, a "dead" mother often continues to help her children through a prayer or a gift. But in stories that allow the mother to truly die, we the listeners can distinguish two sides of the mother that we spend so much childhood energy denying.

Though our mothers may have acted in a nourishing, supportive, protective, self-sacrificing, and empathetic way, we know that every human has a shadowy, hostile side that invades our lives at times and seizes us. It can be reckless, devouring, destructive, undermining, and self-aggrandizing. In fairy tales, this cluster of attitudes, impulses, and behavior patterns is called "the stepmother." In the swans' story, the death of the "good mother" lets us see this shadowy side clearly. Like her mother, the witch, the new Queen possesses moon magic—sideways, dark-winged methods of doing and knowing. This one knows about the longing to de-evolve.

If we apply this story to the family, we could say that the son who becomes ungrounded, flighty, airy, a *puer aeternus* or flying boy, has a father whose male destiny has already suffered a wound. Such a father can succumb to pressure to live a life others want him to live, or some twisting of his nature through religious heavy-handedness, or some squashing of his adventuresomeness by poverty and necessity. When there is this failure in the father, the young males never receive the grounding they need. The father removes himself from his sons, and he is unable to pass down the stiffening of the will, the strengthening of the soul, and the concentration of spirit that the old initiatory male groups worked to pass down to the young men. His entanglement with his own losses and distractions has already caused him to accept the witch. The son—our King—is acting out his father's wound and making it visible.

The witch force may take the shape of a general nervousness in the family, a sense of remoteness, or an unspoken desire that the son lead a higher life than the father is living. In a house where the husband lives no spiritual life or inner life, or the wife is left to take care of the physical or object world by herself, all her busyness becomes a form of *not* doing in her own life. She doesn't pray, she doesn't dance. Not praying and not dancing are forces in the house, forces for not doing— no creation of art, no drawing or painting, no intimate conversation with a spouse, no creation of grief-speech together, no poems written about paths lost or never found, no "depth" in the house. The power of non-doing is like a black hole—it is stronger than any of the galaxies.

I have experienced this grief, and I know it. Men who have lived as swans are aware that all human beings move toward their own fulfillment, and yet the swan man de-evolves. He seems to himself special. He wants special food, a special road without caring whether someone else has no food at all. He believes it is right for him to have what he wants. This callousness fits perfectly the fate that the cowardice of his father led him to. He is remote from all men. He feels himself a man among men for only fifteen minutes a day.

Rainer Maria Rilke, in the following poem, says that if a father leads a religious life, his children will bless him even if he has left the house. But if he refuses to lead a religious life, he remains in the house as a kind of dark force:

Sometimes a man stands up during supper
And walks outdoors, and keeps on walking,
Because of a church that stands somewhere in the East.
And his children say blessings on him, as if he were dead.

And another man, who remains inside his own house,
Dies there, inside the dishes and in the glasses,
So that his children have to go far out into the world
Towards that same church, which he forgot.

The little girl in the story—the seventh child—is most likely an inner female among the male aspects of the young man. If we wanted to call her "the soul," I think it would be all right. When a man has lost his destiny and flown away, his soul remains behind. It is this soul that grieves. It is often through our grieving that we first notice the soul at all. Once the de-evolving shirts fall on the boys, the threads back to their father, the King, are broken.

The scene in which the soul comes upon the forest hut moves me deeply.

My soul must have had this experience often. Perhaps the traveling psyche remembers the scene from dreams. Or it could be that some early civilizations created and lived a ritual around this hut and the after-image lingers. The hut has an eerie quality. It is empty of people, and the objects—the beds, window frames, and rugs—wait for the spirit beings to return. The objects seem filled with some great sorrow and absence, as a body whose spirit has left. We remember that the shaman's body lies on the floor when his soul is flying elsewhere; and his relatives sit about, anxiously waiting, softly beating a drum in this world, holding it down, keeping it stable for the stretched-out, waiting body.

In the story, at dusk six swans fly in through the window where their sister rests stretched out on the floor, waiting. They settle down, blow the feathers off each other's bodies, and stand before her as six young men. In certain Japanese stories the storyteller has a goddess appear from the sky rather than swans. What we call "sky" they call the "celestial realm."

We imagine this little hut as a place of the divine, a temple, some sort of sacred precinct, in which exchanges between the human culture and the divine occur; or, as depth psychology has it, a place full of possibility, awe, and intensity where the archetypes, rising from levels of the psyche utterly inaccessible to the ego, meet, if briefly, with the fearful, frail, attentive human soul.

That meeting, like the Annunciation of the Virgin Mary, trembles with the future; the moment itself is pregnant. All possibilities inherent in our history hover over the roof or behind the half-open doors; the little beds and tables flow with secret life, penetrating the room from the other world. This intensity will prove too much for human beings and when the sister asks to stay with the brothers, they say that robbers live in the hut, too, and if they find her there they will kill her. They tell her they can only be human for one quarter of an hour each day and then they must turn into swans again. They are hardly in the world at all, and they cannot act as protectors for her during the time when they are not human. The girl says she would like to free them. "No. It's too hard. For six years you couldn't speak or laugh, and in that time you'd have to sew six little shirts of starwort. If a single word fell from your lips, all the work would be lost."

Then the brothers turn into swans again and fly away.

What does it mean, this detail: "This is a shelter for robbers; if they come home and find you, they will kill you"? From one point of view, the six boys are themselves the robbers: men like this, who are not earthly and are committed to nothing but their own ease of movement. They live at the edge of the world, and they prowl about the borders of society and take from it more than they give.

The business of living alongside robbers also seems to have a meaning. In *The Golden Ass* by Apuleius, important events happen to the hero when he is in the robbers' cave. And the male hero in the Brothers Grimm's "The Raven" finds himself among robbers. Robbers allow certain greeds to appear naked. Civilized people generally dress them up in pants and suits. Robbers take what they want, without worrying about what is best for the society as a whole; in that way, they resemble complexes that steal psychic energy when they can. A failure complex, a miser's complex, and a sexual complex absorb into their system libido that might have gone to other people, nature, the nation, art. Over the course of the psyche's slow unfolding, we experience what it is like to be among these naked energy-grabbers; their power over us and their ruthlessness become clear. We have experienced the robbers' fanatical energy absorption all our lives without realizing what it was. To know these robbers well and to humanize their complex is difficult and requires labor and constant insight.

So the soul has to leave this small hut where the dangers are too great and the inhuman powers too strong, and go about her work of redeeming the six brothers out of doors. Her tasks have been described to her.

Our whole grasp of the redemption or cure of the swan boys depends on how well we understand the metaphor of their sister's work and her silence. We could say that "recovering your destiny is like living for six years making entire shirts from delicate, easily broken blossoms." That is how it looks when we imagine that our job is to help the King, or the center of the psyche, rediscover our destiny. If we imagine that the task of the soul is to help the young male become human again, recover his ground, that is, to help the young male descend from his compulsive, rather heartless spirituality so that he can commit himself to hunting-gathering, or agriculture, or fatherhood, or husbandhood, or religious fierceness, or love itself, the task is like living for six years without talking or laughing, and it is like making entire shirts from delicate blossoms.

And as for the silence imposed on the soul, we know that the ego activates much of our talking. It does that in order to maintain the illusion of its control. This nervous Prime Minister we call the ego rearranges everything he comes across, claiming it as his own. He pretends to represent the body's position when the body has something else entirely in mind. He represses all interferences from minor beings, fearing they will add to life's chaos. Not to talk for six years would be to experience the interior community as it is: an ecology of complicated and intricate beings, as in the fully developed forest, with no species dominant.

Laughing implies community that we have a share

in; we laugh when the others in our group laugh. Laughter expresses insight, joy, discovery, cruelty, half-apprehended fear, and victory over fear. To be without it is to be without community, to be alone. That is what the soul daughter is asked to experience in our story when she lives without laughing. And she decides that she will redeem her brothers even if she has to give her life for that. Again she walks into the forest. She climbs into a tree to spend the night. The next morning she begins gathering starwort blossoms and practicing her sewing. In sewing, she resembles God, who sewed the thread of spirit into the grass and trees and the vast matter of the universe that surrounds us. By sitting in the tree to do her sewing, the daughter declares herself to be not "earthly" like those Gnostic men and women who at some point direct their attention upward toward the spirit place from which their soul-spark originally fell. The loss of human community soon is dangerous for her.

The King of that area and his retinue are out hunting and discover the girl sitting in the tree. They ask her who she is but she says nothing. *Come down, we won't hurt you.* She answers their questions not with words but by throwing down, piece by piece, all she is wearing except her shift.

This is terrifically interesting. The story says that by not talking we become more naked. Those who have spent weeks or months alone in the woods or in a city know how that can be. At first one feels lonely, but then, wisp by wisp, a sort of cloud attaches itself to our body, and walking about inside it we feel sheltered, hidden, and even nourished. We wake up one morning to say, quite happily, that the prosecuting attorney's evidence is incorrect; even if we have done the crimes we are accused of, we are long ago forgiven. We long for some way to tell that clearly and buoyantly to others. Each day we sense someone asking who we are, and our old answers make no sense at all. Strangely, the question keeps coming up from deep in the psyche: "Who are you?" I once addressed that question in a poem:

After walking about all afternoon,
Inside my lakeside shack, barefoot,
I have grown long and transparent.
By dusk I resemble the sea slug

Who has lived alone doing nothing
For eighteen thousand years!

In ancient China, Wang Wei, who had retired from his civil service career, and a younger poet, P'ei Ti, practiced writing comparison poems while each of them lived alone in an isolated river valley. Wan Wei wrote:

The mountain receives the last sunshine of fall.
Flocks fly off following the first that leaves.
Occasionally something emerald flashes in the trees.
The evening dark has nowhere to settle down.

P'ei Ti answered:

Settling down at dusk from the dome of light
Bird voices get mingled with the river sounds.
The path beside the river winds off into the distance,
Joy of solitude, will you ever come to an end?

The soul in nakedness and solitude convinces us that the person we truly are has been obscured and that this has been going on through many centuries and life-times. Great grief then overtakes us.

But as we live in this grief we understand that "the King of that area has come near" and, in comparison to that gift, our grief seems small, and we let what happens happen. The girl's beauty touches the King's heart. He likes her reserved presence and he marries her.

This tells us that when the soul vows to redeem the de-evolved "brothers," these brothers are not the only ones who benefit from the disciplines it practices. The soul itself gets closer to the King, who is the center of the psyche (that definition leaves us room for imagina-tion and interpretation). I think that the one who gets in touch with the center of his or her psyche is lucky, as presumably life at the edges means a constant battle with complexes, fragmentation, distraction, and psychic poison, as well as anxiety and depression. In our story the soul meets the King and finds that he is in love with her! The King, like God in certain cultures, is lacking something; he needs completion by something tender and human. Here, it is a tongue-tied, obsessed being whom the King loves. But just getting in touch with the center of one's psyche does not solve anything. The experience can get buried by the duties and necessities of adulthood. People "forget" and head back to the provinces at the edge of life.

And, we note, even when things are going well with us, it isn't long before negative energies are stirred up. The King's mother, herself a kind of witch, invents crimes for her daughter-in-law, which lead to a trial for her life, and the young one is condemned to fire. Witches seem to have curious links back to our early childhood. Maybe the "witch" accuses a mother of having done exactly what it wants to do itself, namely, eat a competitor. Perhaps we spent considerable energy framing our mother and hoping our father would then abandon her; and this framing is a habit now, and we apply it also to the "spiritual mother" and, through that framing, find a reason to be secular, or at least to avoid praising any feminine spirit. Perhaps this extrapolation is too elaborate, but the witch's accusations do seem to belong to our early personal history.

And it echoes far, far back also in our cultural history. Celtic myths in written form date to the second half of the eleventh century and in oral form probably go back another thousand years or more into the Celtic past. In one, the Prince, after many adventures, marries Rhiannon, a name we recognize as belonging to a Celtic goddess. Somewhere along the way the storyteller begins calling the Prince a King. While the King's first son is being born, the six waiting women fall asleep. The Queen does, too. When they wake and find the baby gone, the women smear the sleeping Queen's face with the blood of a puppy. The Queen pleads with them to tell the truth for their own sakes, if not for hers. The King's counselors direct him to put the Queen to death, but he will not. She is given penance—seven years during which she must carry people as if she were a horse, and tell everyone the story of that night.

The Celtic story suggests that there was a ritual disappearance of some holy child, involving six women plus the mother to make seven. There was animal sacrifice and probably the ritual drinking of blood. The old tradition, still alive among healers in Africa, says that drinking the blood of a ritually sacrificed animal puts the drinker in touch with the ancestors. Rhiannon remains with the ancestors by becoming a storyteller and by carrying, so to speak, the burden of the tribe.

In "The Six Swans," the theme of the holy boy or

holy girl who needs to disappear from his or her parents' house and be brought elsewhere to live among
strangers does not figure directly in our story, but the
bloody mouth, the accusation, the husband's resistance,
and the final penance remain. If we consider that all
figures in "The Six Swans" represent parts of a single
psyche, and if we take that psyche to be that of a young
male who has suffered a disaster that has made him spiritual in a mechanical or nonhuman way, then what
meaning is there to be found in the bloody mouth and
the accusations about it?

The male parts that have become spiritual too
quickly, ascending too early and leaving the world
behind, can only be redeemed by "the seventh," that
part that sews shirts, lives in nature, and cannot talk or
laugh. The "shirts" call attention to the heart and chest
area. And starwort, being a low-lying flower with star-
shaped blossoms, unites sky and ground, mind and
body, air and earth, stars and vegetation, the heavenly
and the practical. When sewn together with the univer-
sal thread, all the polarities will come together.

The labor of making shirts is like the labor one
finds in yoga practices, meditation, and concentrated

psychotherapy. It is physical labor of the type that monks and Sufi students undertake while they study God, the daily tasks that Buddhists accept so that their meditation room remains spotless, their clothes simple and clean; they "intend" each action they take.

But our story seems to go one step further. If the witch, who represents some tremendous intelligence that knows all about the most intricate processes of growth, accuses the redeemer of having eaten her children, the chances are she has. She has eaten her children *and* they are still alive somewhere. Their simultaneous disappearance and presence somewhere else parallel the situation of the first King's children, who have disappeared from the castle, though they remain alive elsewhere. This particularly parallels the fate of the six brothers, who disappeared entirely as human beings, namely in their hut that has six beds, six chairs, six chamber pots, six plates, and so on. Eating one's children would mean psychologically forgetting about certain strengths they represent in us, losing touch with our spiritual life for years, losing fruits of long labor finished, as when Gerard Manley Hopkins omitted the effort to publish his poems, or Emily Dickinson didn't mention to her relatives the thousand or so poems among her private papers, which were found after she died. This sacrifice (for it does resemble sending something that is alive into stagnation, or immobility, or death) seems to be necessary if the star-sewing process is to work all the way through. I don't believe this sacrifice is made entirely consciously, and so the metaphor of the Queen's having "eaten her children in her sleep" is a good metaphor for it, and her not defending herself, even with sign language or some sort of dance, seems to fit. To focus all the power required to complete her redemptive task, she has to eat her children and not eat them, and endure the pity, disgust, and disfiguring fantasies from her own distress, right up to the moment of the fire. Then the Queen can say aloud to the King (who was overwhelmed by what he had seen), *Beloved, I am innocent.* It is important to note that the King is overjoyed that their offspring are still alive. He wanted the novel finished, the poems published, the labors for the love of God not to be discarded.

The story says, to the great joy of the King, the children came out of their hiding place, the brothers were restored to their bodies, and the witch, for her punishment, was tied to the now empty stake and burned to ashes. It is important to see that this is not a story of a woman saving a man. There are no men or women in this story. The being who does the sewing and keeps the silence could just as well be called "the seventh." She is the seventh, magical, hardworking, love-motivated, serving, tree-loving, poem-producing, art-producing, modest, well-mannered, powerful part of the psyche that understands the primitive value of sacrifice. She has not been ruined by the disasters that happened to her as they happen to us all. And at the end of the story the King and Queen live with her brothers in happiness for all time to come.

* * *

Obviously the male and female psyches have some fundamental structure in common, and this story describes, give or take a little, the healing operations that are as independent of time or place as the operations on the molecular level, when electrons jump a ring up or down. Or they are like the necessities of nest-building, or the manner in which the octopus makes an undersea house from stones. It is the same in all oceans. And yet

"The Six Swans" carries, I think, some of the anguish of being a man or, more freely, of being a certain sort of man. The de-evolutionary experience described in "The Six Swans" does not happen to all men. Percy Shelley was one of those to whom it happened:

> My soul is an enchanted boat,
> Which, like a sleeping swan, doth float
> Upon the silver waves of thy sweet singing.

During the Middle Ages the swan was imagined as the son of those sorts of women who perform intercourse with their husbands on their wedding night, and never again. After that the mother transfers her libido to the son, the swan-son, and away from the boy's father: and all such transfers suggest physical or psychic incest. As soon as he notices that he has replaced his father in the tournament of love, the boy picks up, through the power of fantasy-contamination, the ancient longing of his mother. She has a double hold on the boy and her longings disturb the son's later relationships with women, as Yeats's mother-longing, described by him in "The Wanderings of Oisin," disturbed his life until he was over fifty, perhaps even longer. When Yeats was twenty-three he fantasized having his daily world with a passive woman called Niamh:

> And on the shores were many boats
> With bending sterns and bending bows,
> And carven figures on their prows
> Of bitterns, and fish-eating stoats,
> And swans with their exultant throats:

Later the two of them find a strange place where monstrous beings lie sleeping, "naked and gleaming":

> And by them were arrow and war-axe, arrow and shield and blade;
> And dew-blanched horns, in whose hollow a child of
>   three years old
> Could sleep on a couch of rushes, and all inwrought and inlaid,
> And more comely than man can make them with bronze and silver
>   and gold.

> And each of the huge, white creatures was huger than fourscore men;
> The tops of their ears were feathered, their hands were the claws of
>   birds,

And, shaking the plumes of the grasses and the leaves of the
    mural glen,
The breathing came from those bodies, long warless, grown whiter
    than curds.

Yeats and Rilke were the two poets who described most vividly the swan man or swan god who made love to a curiously passive woman and fathered Helen, the moon-woman. There is a sort of triangle of swan, moon, and moon-boy.

Yeats for his part often accepted a partial identification of himself and the swan. In "The Tower," as he thinks of writing his will, he offers to younger men his pride:

Pride, like that of the morn . . .
Or that of the hour
When the swan must fix his eye
Upon a fading dream,
Float out upon a long
Last reach of glittering stream
And there sing his last song.

Yeats's beloved Lady Gregory had swans at her

country estate and Yeats, noticing that it was nineteen years since he first saw them, is aware that, now being fifty-three, part of him is no longer swan, has become human, vulnerable, open to grief. Yeats wrote in "The Wild Swans of Coole":

I have looked upon those brilliant creatures,
And now my heart is sore.
All's changed since I, hearing at twilight,
The first time on this shore,
The bell-beat of their wings above my head,
Trod with a lighter tread.

Unwearied still, lover by lover,
They paddle in the cold
Companionable streams or climb the air;
Their hearts have not grown old;
Passion or conquest, wander where they will,
Attend upon them still.

We'll call the swan bewitchment the first stage, that of leaving with some complaisant woman for some magic land where he would possess this woman exclusively, as we all once possessed, or were possessed by our mothers in the womb, and live in a kind of Paradise, though separated from the human. During this time Yeats, as the young male, remains passive in his fantasies; he endures what happens to him, as the six swan boys in our story remain receptive. They do not plot their freedom themselves and live in a kind of birdlike resignation that can last for years.

From Yeats's poem we can reconstruct a little of how Yeats felt at that very early time in his life. "The Six Swans" is brilliant, and yet it works primarily to make us aware of what "the daughter" feels, what the first and second King feel, what the witch feels. Did Yeats free himself from the swan-boy hut through his poems? Probably. The poems the soul creates are, in fact, a kind of heart-shirt, at the other end of things from what the witch made for her magic.

But how does the swan boy in the hut actually feel about his enchantment? I lived in the sea hut for many years and each detail seems to me precise. He feels lonely, helpless, and angry. He feels himself somehow to have acquired a high destiny that doesn't allow him to express anger, and so the anger falls below, where he

cannot retrieve it, the evidence of it appearing acciden-
tally and confusing him. He knows well that something
bad has happened to him, but not what it is, or who
caused it, or why. He is remote, distant, elevated, intellectual, cold, self-conscious, awake in the cold heavens.
For fifteen minutes a day he is warm and human, and
you have to catch him at that time if you want to talk
to him.

The swan boy's father loved him but let the witch
find him. The remoteness from the father means that
the boy is cut off from the male support and knowledge
that lie beyond the father, or in the unoccupied space
between himself and his father.

The young male in his swan hut does not feel his
swan nature as luck then, nor as an aspect of happiness.
His transformed nature draws certain women to him,
who find his unearthliness attractive and a contrast
perhaps to an obsession in their own families with the
daily round. His nature draws people who long for spirit
and hope for a spirit companion. But the young male's
automatic body system, to which he devotes much attention, his moods, and his thought-factory, usually make
him feel himself mechanical, so he is not attentive

spiritually to others and does not have enough will to move powerfully forward against inertia.

Many women mistake the unexpressed grief of the young male in this circumstance for a congenitally cold personality, or they believe he is carrying hostility toward women, or a calculated and conspiratorial cunning that results in damage to others. If a woman tries to help such a man, she will be wasting her time.

It is the activities of his own soul that he will have to turn to in order to find his way back to himself, keeping a long silence from both talk and laughter, not looking to others to find himself reflected. And he will have to give constant and honest attention to the minutest workings of his own heart. With such attention to those practices, he will again be able to be connected to the earth at last and to earn the return of his own humanity.

TWO

THE FROG PRINCE

IN EARLIER TIMES, WHEN WISHING STILL HELPED A TRAVELER who sat down next to a well, there lived a King whose daughters were all beautiful, but the youngest was so beautiful that the sun itself, which has seen so much, was astonished whenever it shone on her face. Close by the King's castle stood a great dark forest.

There under an old lime tree was a well. When the day was very warm, the King's child went out into the forest and sat down by the side of the well. When she was bored she took a golden ball, threw it up high, and caught it. This ball was her favorite plaything.

Now it so happened that on one occasion the Princess's golden ball did not fall into the little hand that she held up for it, but onto the ground beyond, and it rolled straight into the water. The King's daughter followed it with her eyes, but it vanished, and the well was deep, so deep that the bottom could not be seen. At this she began to cry. She cried louder and louder and could not be comforted. As she cried someone said to her, "Why are you crying, King's daughter?" She looked around and saw a frog stretching its big, ugly head up from the well.

"You cry as if your heart were breaking. What's wrong?"

The girl said in a small voice, "Well, you see, I've lost my golden ball. It's fallen into the well."

"Do you want it back?"

"Yes. Yes, I do! I want it back."

"What will you give me if I bring up your plaything?"

"Oh, I'll give you anything! Anything you like. I am a Princess. You can have my jewels. I'll give you my rings. I'll even give you the little crown that I have."

"What good would your crown and your jewels be to me? But if you will let me sit on your little chair, and eat from your little golden plate, drink from your little golden cup, and sleep in your little bed, in other words, let me be your companion and play-fellow, I will go down and bring you your golden ball again."

"Yes, yes," she replied. But to herself she said, *This is ridiculous. He is just an old splasher. He can't be a companion to a Princess.*

So the frog popped back down into the water and came up with the golden ball in his mouth. He spat it out on the grass. She picked up the ball and ran right back to her father's castle. The frog hopped after, calling, "Wait! Wait!" But she ran very fast and there was nothing he could do but go back to his well.

That evening, the Princess was having dinner with her father in the dining room of the castle. A little knock came at the door. The Princess went out to see. "It's the frog!" She closed the door quickly and sat down with her father.

"Why are you looking so pale?"

"It's nothing."

"Go ahead. Tell me!"

"Well, I lost my golden ball in the well and I wanted it back. Then this frog appeared and said that he would bring it to me if I would let him sit on my little chair, eat from my little plate, drink from my little cup, sleep in my little bed."

"Did you promise that?"

"Yes."

"What is promised should be performed."

The Princess didn't want to let the frog come in, but she could hear it calling.

She went to the door.

"Princess, listen to me. Have you forgotten the words you spoke to me by the cool water? Open the door."

She opened the door for him and he jumped up the marble stairs to the dining room—*squissh, squissh, squoossh, squoossh.* The Princess lifted him up on the table and he began to eat a little bit from her plate. She instantly lost her appetite. But it wasn't over yet, because after supper came bedtime. When she started up the stairs to her room, the frog said, "Don't forget to take me along with you."

"This is so ridiculous," she said.

Her father scolded her. "If someone helped you when you were in trouble, it's not right to despise that person."

So she took the frog by two fingers, brought him upstairs, and put him on the corner of the bed. She changed for bed, slipped inside her smooth, clean sheets, and laid her head on her freshly aired pillow.

"Aren't you going to bring me to your pillow? If you don't, I'll tell your father." That was too much for her. She reached down, grabbed the frog, and threw him against the wall as hard as she could—*fffaaoow!*

A handsome Prince appeared.

"Thank you," he said. "I was turned into a frog by an old sorcerer," he said. "You are the only one who could have released me. Now we can return to my father's kingdom and be married!"

She said, "I like that idea."

The next morning, a carriage with eight white horses pulled up. So now there were four beings: the Princess, the Prince who was the frog, the carriage—which in old times people thought of as the body—and a being called Faithful Henri, who rode on a step at the back of the carriage. These four then set out. When they were a mile or so out of town, they heard a twang from something breaking, and the Prince said, "Is this the wheel of the carriage breaking?" And Faithful Henri said, "All the time that you were a frog and speechless, all the time that you were living in the dark, I felt so much grief that I had to wear three iron bands around my chest to keep my heart from breaking. You just heard the first band break."

They went a few more miles and they heard another loud sound, and the Prince said, "Is that the carriage wheel breaking?" Faithful Henri said, "It is not the carriage wheel breaking. All the time that you were reduced to a frog, unable to be a human being, unable to speak, I felt so much grief that I had to put three iron bands around my chest to keep my heart from breaking. You just heard the second breaking."

After another mile or so, they heard a similar sound. The Prince said, "Is that the carriage wheel breaking?" Faithful Henri said, "No. All the time that you were cold and alone, unable to be with others, I felt so much grief for you that I put three iron bands around my chest. You just heard the third band break."

The three of them kept on in the carriage until they came to the kingdom of the Prince's father. It was time to be married. They had a wonderful wedding. There was so much joy that the neighbors and the castle people danced for three or four days. The wedding pair gave food to the poor and sent gifts to all the people who were sick and suffering in that area. In fact, the wedding was so wonderful, it has been talked about ever since.

* * *

So let's look at what the story says. If the story says that the two got married, it means that the male and female parts inside the single psyche are united, and the marriage is an image for that unity. In this story we can imagine the movement toward unity in stages. Let's say there are seven of them: loss of the golden ball; the Princess's promise; learning to live with the frog; the Princess has had enough; the frog becomes a Prince; Faithful Henri is released from grief; and the Prince and the Princess are married.

The golden ball suggests the sun, an integrated, round, golden energy, but also that kind of wholeness that we had in us when we were three or four or five years old. To some extent, the golden ball is the energy that radiates in all directions off a young child. When you take that child and force him to sit still and become socialized, a lot of that energy is suppressed, and by the time the child is eighteen, the golden ball is down in the water. When this happens to you and you get the feeling that something is wrong, then you spend the next ten or fifteen years trying to get the ball back.

Here's a poem that touches on that loss:

The fall has come, clear as the eyes of chickens.
Awkward sounds come from the sea,
Sounds of muffled oarlocks
And swampings in lonely bays,
Surf crashing on unchristened shores,
And the wash of tiny snail shells in the wandering gravel.

My body also is lost or wandering: I know it,
As I cradle a pen, or walk down a stair
Holding a cup in my hand,
Not breaking into the pastures that lie in the sunlight.
This sloth is far inside the body,
The sloth of the body lost among the wandering stones of kindness.

Something homeless is looking on the long roads,
A dog lost since midnight, a box-elder

Bug who doesn't know
Its walls are gone, its house
Burnt. Even the young sun is lost,
Wandering over earth as the October night comes down.

I wrote that when I was about thirty-four, I think. Walking downstairs, I had that feeling that something was wrong. Some great loss had happened. Kabir, a Hindu poet from India, says he has lost a "small ruby":

The small ruby everyone wants has fallen out on the road.
Some say it is East of us, others West of us.
Some say "among primitive earth rocks," others "in the deep
*   waters."*
Kabir's instinct told him it was inside, and what it was worth,
And he wrapped it up carefully in his heart cloth.

As the story opens, the Princess is disturbing her securely walled castle-world by playing with her golden ball. Some would say she is playing with all her possibilities. It is that playfulness and her error of letting the ball fall into the well that bring the frog into the story. The frog is a natural choice for its ability to transform from tadpole to adult frog. Why not to a Prince then?

I was brought up to believe that the golden ball was in the hands of angels. In the story we learn that it is up to us to retrieve our own potential through our instinct, sometimes the swampy dark side, the ugly frog side, which could bring the ball back but will insist on something in return. I like to think of those four frog gods of Egypt who were said to live in the time of chaos and primeval waters even before the creation of land and light. It was from those waters that the sun god rose in the form of a great golden ball.

The frog in the story comes up out of the other-worldly well with a golden ball and demands something in return for what he returns to land. He wants the nice, orderly, and beautiful Princess to take him into her father's nice, orderly castle to live closely with his ugly, slimy self. She would prefer not to. But it is really an all-or-nothing situation. Either she allows him to go plopping up the stone stairs to her room and lets him settle down on her nice clean pillow, or she lives out her aversion, dividing things, judging them and removing herself to the side of order and predictability, as if she had never heard of the swampy little fellow. If she does this, she doesn't get the return of the perfect sphere of golden metal that is so dear to her. And that sphere contains all the potential of land and light she has yet to realize. Luckily, her father reminds her of her promise, and if she accepts his advice, she will be open to frog-energy that's outside the small circle of her delight.

In Buddhist and Hindu literature there is a lot of discussion of the worth of this golden ball. You also find it mentioned in a few of our poets—in Gerard Manley Hopkins, Wordsworth, Blake. But Westerners don't describe the stages of the promise very clearly, nor is the loss clearly defined. People in the sixties and seventies had the optimistic belief that if they just loved each other, everything would be wonderful. But they also took it for granted that life is for growth. Rilke described this growth as moving in spirals. He says:

I am circling around God, around the ancient tower,
and I have been circling for a thousand years,

and I still don't know if I am a falcon,
or a storm, or a great song.

Someone in the Princess's place will have to leave her aversions behind if she is to have any hope of learning what her life could be made of. It's all right, though—she is probably a bit curious about what will happen when this frog moves into the castle with her. The Princess's experience so far has been only in the father-ordered world. A good way to learn about something so completely foreign as a frog is to get into a conversation with it, though he's not easy to talk to, not a courtier in her father's court. He does know how she can heal what has put her in the awkward position of not having the golden ball in hand.

Most people, when the frog says, *I can return the ball,* will say, *I do not need you.* But the frog insists. He wants her to join him. He wants to join her. He wants to eat from her little plate and so forth, and sometimes this closeness nauseates her. He is not a brilliant thinker. He likes to splash around in the muddy water of feeling repressed by castle-dwellers. If she lets herself know him, the Princess will open into a new dimension, know more of her own nature. She will muse about her own chaotic and murky aspects, and she will be emotionally alive, as happens in so many good fairy stories. This is not to say she will see herself in a new form, but rather she will find some ancient part, perhaps allowing herself to see into the blind spot that developed when her mother disappeared.

The frog in the story makes demands and more demands. He even asks to be set on the Princess's little pillow. Outrageous! The Princess has had enough. She throws him against the wall. In very early religions a sacrifice precedes transformation. This is not a description of such a rite, but it might be a reference to an earlier view of the way those things worked. As for me, when I saw the darkness in me beginning to come forward, I wrote this poem, welcoming the new view of things:

CHINESE TOMB GUARDIANS

Oh yes, I love you, book of my confessions,
Where what was swallowed, pushed away, sunken,
Driven down, begins to rise from the earth
Once more, and the madness and rage from the wells.

The buried is still buried, like cows who eat
*In a collapsed strawpile all winter to get out.**

Something inside me is still imprisoned in winter straw,
Or far back in the mountain where Charlemagne sleeps,
Or under the water, hard to get to, guarded by women.
Enough rises from that place to darken my poems;
Perhaps too much; and what remains down there
Makes a faint glow in the dead leaves.

I am less than half risen. I see how carefully
I have covered my tracks as I wrote,
How well I have brushed over the past with my tail.
Faces look at me from the shallow waters,
Where I have pushed them down—
Father and mother pushed into the dark.

*This image needs some explanation. In Minnesota in the old days we had straw piles that the cows would eat. Once in a while one would eat so far that the straw pile would collapse on top of it. The farmer would go out in the morning and the cow was gone. Actually, the cow was inside the straw pile. It would just keep eating and three months later come out the other side. Enough snow would melt to give it water. The farmers never worried; they always knew the cow would survive.

What am I in my ambition and loneliness?
I am the dust that fills the cracks on the ocean floor.
Floating like the stingray, used to the weight
Of the ocean floor, retreating to a cave,
I live as a lizard or a winged shark,
Darting out at times to wound others, or get food.

How do we know that the hidden will ever rise?
How do we know that the buried will be revealed?
Some beings get used to life underneath.
Some dreams do not want to move into the light.
Some want to, but they can't; they can't make their way out,
Because someone is guarding the posts of the door.

Have you seen those Chinese tomb guardians
Left at the closed door? They stand with one knee raised;
They half-stand, half-dance, half-rage, half-shout—
Hot-tempered muscle-bulgers, big-kneed brow-bulgers.
They scowl for eternity at the half-risen.
What do you have that can get past them?

Grimm recorded the very old Germanic version of this story. This version is adapted from "The Frog

Prince" as found in the Pantheon *Grimm's Fairy Tales*. In other versions the frog demands to have his head cut off and then he is transformed, or he simply hangs out with the Princess until the transformation takes place, or in the Italian version the kiss the Princess gives him transforms him. Ours is the Northern European version and I like it much better, the little shock you feel when instead of kissing the frog she throws it against the wall. The frog form as it was is destroyed and then transforms into a marvelous Prince form. We ask ourselves whether this old story refers to a sacrifice of a young male to refresh the King. (An earlier name for the story was "The Frog King.") The story's setting in the Pantheon telling is a castle, a refinement added in the nineteenth century. Earlier versions begin in mysterious evocative forests that hint at the otherworldly divinities inhabiting them. The old Germanic goddess Holle, who occasionally turned into a frog, might be there, and Nerthus, too, who, when she was washed by her slaves, had them drowned in a hidden lake connected with mysteries and sacrifice.

This story is an observation of the frog's darker maneuvers. Well, maybe that's more indictment than the frog deserves, but no Princess wants to devote her-self completely to the subterranean watery world. She can't live forever in the losses she has known—of her mother and of her nice-girl-Princess-world. Her blow against the frog's suggestion had the effect of the frog's becoming human. When we really have lived with the hidden and buried and cold-blooded, when we see who we are and understand something of what it means to have pockets of the prehuman in our hidden nature, then finally it's possible to say, "Okay. You're always there. But you have to stop trying to have it all your way. I've had enough. You can't possibly take over my whole life."

Then even the cold-blooded alien part of ourselves gets a bit more human. Here's a poem about the moment just before that happens. The poem began when it was getting dark out and I hadn't noticed. I opened a door and found moonlight flooding the whole room.

I

After many strange thoughts,
Thoughts of distant harbors, and new life,
I came in and found the moonlight lying on the floor.

II

Outside it covers the trees like pure sound,
The sound of tower bells, or of water moving under the ice,
The sound of the deaf hearing through the bones of their heads.

III

We know the road; as the moonlight
Lifts everything, so in a night like this
The road goes on ahead, it is all clear.

When the frog becomes human, after the Princess's determined act has released him from the sorcerer's spell, he wants to marry her. A footman, Faithful Henri, attends the pair on their way to the father's kingdom. It is strange for Faithful Henri, a familiar fairy-tale character, to turn up so late in a story. This time he says he has been carrying so much of the Prince's grief during his enchantment that it took three iron bands around his chest to keep his heart from breaking. It was the grief of having no speech, no way of talking things over, no heart-to-heart, that made things so sad for him.

Some traditions indicate that this is a story of

different states of a woman's masculine side—the Germanic goddess Holle, who shifts sometimes into frog form, for example, is female. Others believe the narrative follows the progress of a man's feminine soul. I like the latter, because the sudden and final act that transforms the Prince feels, to me, male in tone, and a male retainer (Faithful Henri) has been able to carry the sustained grief of the Prince's enchantment only with the help of three iron (from Mars) bands. Henri's powerful grief will be fertile now, as this poem suggests:

What is sorrow for? It is a storehouse
Where we store wheat, barley, corn and tears.
We step to the door on a round stone,
And the storehouse feeds all the birds of sorrow.
And I say to myself: Will you have
Sorrow at last? Go on, be cheerful in autumn,
Be stoic, yes, be tranquil, calm;
Or in the valley of sorrows spread your wings.

Though the frog was basically a royal being, his grief at becoming a frog was still mute. Faithful Henri himself, on the other hand, is not young, and he knows what his heart has to say and has listened to the heart of the Prince while he was enchanted. His witnessing requires great faithfulness. And when all three of Faithful Henri's bands are broken he can let his compassion flow out toward the Prince, but still he doesn't interfere. This is very important. He allows things to go on, to take their own way. He's gone unnoticed for many years, watching the direction things were moving. That was fine with him. He knows about the frog and at the same time he's riding behind eight white horses leading the carriage. He is both high and low. Divine and human. But in our civilization the *higher* part of him has gotten tangled up with the mind and with the ego. We must be very suspicious of the ego when it tells us we are among the *high*. The kind of intellectual work the ego does has a fixed quality, and it doesn't allow itself to be loose enough to say, as this story does, *Yes, that's great, you're playing with your golden ball; but you're missing a whole other world*. The ego's kind of intellect avoids our immense suffering and pain and it runs around like the well-known monkey trying to keep us going. Love gets trampled in the rush. That's why myth is so helpful. It helps us recognize the intelligence of the body, of the heart, and of the whole being that is, at its center, a golden ball. We get to see the difference between what the ego wants and an enduring love, like the love of Faithful Henri, who won't give up grieving the Prince's enchantment until it's completely broken and the Prince is free. We should all be lucky enough to know love like that.

A man and a woman sit near each other, and they do not long
At this moment to be older, or younger, or born
In any other nation, or any other time, or any other place.
They are content to be where they are, talking or not talking.
Their breaths together feed someone whom we do not know.
The man sees the way his fingers move;
He sees her hands close around a book she hands to him.
They obey a third body that they share in common.
They have promised to love that body.
Age may come; parting may come; death will come!
A man and a woman sit near each other;
As they breathe they feed someone whom we do not know,
Someone we know of, whom we have never seen.

THREE

THE LINDWORM

A KING AND QUEEN RULED OVER VAST LANDS AND longed for an offspring but didn't have one. So one day the Queen was thinking about her situation and walking in the woods, and she met an old lady there who said, "Why do you look so sad?"

"Ah, you see, I'm longing for a child and we haven't had one."

"Oh, it's not a big problem. I can tell you what to do so that you can have two sons and not just one."

"Just tell me. I'll do whatever you say."

The old lady said, "You must listen carefully and

follow my instructions. Tonight, fill your bath as usual, but when you're done with it, throw the water under the tub and then you'll find two onions. Peel them carefully and eat them, and pretty soon you're going to have two boys."

The Queen was delighted. She went straight home, filled her bath, and the two onions appeared as soon as she threw the water under the tub. Seeing them, she forgot what the old woman told her and she ate the first onion whole, peel and all. Then she remembered, *Oh yes. Peel the onion.* So she did and she ate the second one, too.

After several months she said to her husband the King, "I think we're going to need a midwife." He was very happy. The midwife came in the ninth month when the Queen was giving birth. She and the Queen were alone in the chamber. The first thing that came out was a little snake about six inches long. The midwife said, *Well, I don't think it's worth mentioning*, and she threw it out the window. And then the second one came and it was a beautiful, shining boy. He was gorgeous. Golden hair. A wonderful child. And the subjects sent gifts. Everybody rejoiced. It was marvelous.

So things went on. The boy got to be about twenty and that was the time to be married. So the father and mother decided he should find someone to marry and he should search for her in a different kingdom. The boy started out with his two horses and his gilded carriage to search for a bride and bring her back to his parents' castle. He got about three miles out and all of a sudden the horses screamed and stopped the carriage. In front of them in the middle of the road lay a huge serpent.

"Argaaaahhhhhhhh. Where are you going?"

"As if it is any business of yours. But I'm going out to look for a bride."

"Noooo," the serpent roared. "A bride for me before a bride for you!" The horses struggled to break free, frightened by the horrible sound. "I am the eldest son. Eldest sons marry first."

The golden boy turned around and drove home. He said to his father, "I met somebody at the crossroads today. Do you know anything about an older son?"

Father said, "Nooo."

So the royal son waited a couple of weeks and set out again. He got about three miles out of town, and there, right in the middle of the road, was the same awful serpent, bigger than ever.

"Rooooarah. A bride for me before a bride for you. Eldest sons marry first." The horses all coughed at the horrible stench on the serpent's breath. So the royal boy hurried home and said to his father, "I think there's something out there. Let's ask Mother."

And they went to her and said, "Do you know anything about an elder son?"

"No." Because she didn't know about that one.

But the midwife was still alive. They went to her and they said, "Something has turned up which leads us to believe that there may have been an earlier child. Do you know anything about this?"

"Yes, I do. The first one to come out was a little snake about six inches long."

"Really! What did you do?"

"I hardly thought it was worth mentioning. It was so small, I just threw it out."

* * *

So now we know that the snake has grown up in nature, and it was certainly quite large, and not happy about being thrown out the window while the royal boy was safe inside the castle, getting all the goodies.

The parents realized that what the Lindworm said was true. And he was also right that custom dictates that the first son marries first. So what could they do? They searched around and found a woman who was willing to marry him. The King declared, *The marriage will be tomorrow.* And in this culture it was also true that the bride and groom sleep together the night before the wedding, then wed in the morning.

So that night the King and Queen gave the Lindworm a room in the castle.

When he came out to greet the bride-to-be, she was standing there all alone. He wrapped his tail around her, took her into the bedroom, and shut the door.

In the morning the King and the Queen went into the chamber—but they saw that only the snake was there. It seemed that during the night he had eaten his bride. The royal Prince waited for a time, then climbed into his royal carriage and headed out to seek a bride. But again, at the crossroads the serpent reared up in his path, looking very angry.

"Rooooar. A bride for me before a bride for you. I'm the eldest son. I'm not married."

The Prince turned around and hurried home to confer with his parents. They had searched far and wide and come up with another candidate for marriage with the Lindworm. Again the bride-to-be stood outside the door of the Lindworm's room. He wrapped his tail around her, too, and took her into the bedroom and shut the door. The following morning the King and Queen went to the chamber. Again only the snake was there. The bride-to-be was completely gone. No trace of her was left.

Now at the edge of the kingdom there lived a stepmother who was terribly annoyed that her husband's daughter was so beautiful, much more beautiful than her own daughter was. Over time, this stepmother had conceived a hatred for the beautiful stepdaughter, so that when she heard the news from the King's palace that there was a serpent who ate each woman who agreed to marry him, and who was now demanding another beautiful new bride, she went to the King and casually remarked that her stepdaughter had offered to wed the Lindworm. *So that the royal Prince will be able to travel abroad and find his bride,* she said. The King and Queen agreed to try out this new candidate, but they were a little sorrowful.

When the messengers arrived to fetch the third young girl, she was terribly frightened. She knew her wicked stepmother had made the arrangement in order that the Lindworm would devour her, as he had devoured the others. She begged to be allowed to spend one more night at her father's house. Permission was given, and she went to her mother's grave. There she wept bitterly, telling everything about the stepmother's hatred and about being promised to the Lindworm. She cried out to her mother and after a long time fell asleep on the earth. In the morning she woke just as the sun was rising. It was the day she was to meet her bride-groom.

When she arrived at the castle she remembered the words her mother had spoken to her while she slept. She asked at the castle for a pot of lye, three scrubbing brushes, and a pot of milk to be set by the fire. Then she dressed herself in seven clean, snow-white shifts. As soon as the Lindworm carried her into the chamber where they were to spend the night, he commanded her:

"Undress yourself."

"You undress yourself first!"

No one had ever uttered a command in the Lindworm's presence before. He was so surprised that he did what she demanded. He struggled and struggled his way out of his "enameled skin."

In response, the bride took off one of her snow-white shifts.

"Undress yourself," he said again.

"You first!"

So he fought his way out of his second skin. It was painful to remove it and he suffered very much with the pain.

They continued in this manner until there were seven skins and seven shifts on the floor and the Lindworm lay in a white formless mass alongside them. That is what a man fears most—lying in a formless white mass on the bedroom floor. But the stepdaughter took one of the three scrub brushes her mother had told her to use, dipped it in lye, and, even though he was raw, she scrubbed him with all her might. She wore out all three brushes before she was finished. But by that time she had uncovered a Prince much lovelier than his younger brother. And she was more than content to marry him. The King and Queen attended the wedding, the Lindworm inherited the kingdom, and the younger brother went off to another kingdom where he found his bride and his fortune as well.

And they all lived happily ever after.

* * *

In the Lindworm story, there is infertility in the land. It's a theme that tells the reader that the two people at the very center of a kingdom, the King and Queen themselves, can't coax fecundity or renewal into their lives. They are not interested in anything wild and nothing from the under-worldly part of life, which includes the great serpent that's soon to be roaming around outside the castle and crashing through the forests, doing whatever it pleases. This situation has antecedents. Myths several centuries before the Common Era told of the great serpent Python, who kept fertility from the land, partly because Leto, his mother, was not allowed to give birth in any place where the sun shone. Python was an earth-dragon and would normally have brought fecundity with him, as snakes have been thought to do, but not in this case. Beyond Python, there are many, many serpent fairy stories. Even Eros, the god of love, in some versions of his story begins as a serpent and Lord of the Underworld, and eventually takes his part in a resurrection story, as the Lindworm does.

But who or what nurtured the Lindworm after he was thrown away? His predecessor, Python, found sustenance at the navel of the world, but that only lasted until the sun god Apollo killed him and took over that navel for himself. The Lindworm had grown so big, so fast, that maybe he was nurtured at that same navel. The Apollo-like second son in our story has golden hair and a conscious way about him that helps him accept his parents' claim that their choices for him are better than anything he would choose for himself. He clings, in his obedience, to their wishes. If they think he should marry, he will do just that.

The Lindworm, the elder son, lives at the outer edges of his father's territory. It's in the wild that he learns what's going on in the land. He is aware of the fatigue of the royal energy. He knows firsthand that the enervation in the kingdom comes from ignoring the chthonic world, tossing it out the window, imagining it to be so small and insignificant that its presence needn't be mentioned in the royal household.

It was through heroic acts that Apollo wiped out the chthonic Python at the center of the world, wielding his weapons and his superlatively conscious mind to destroy the place where the dark and fertile thrive. Afterward, his light shone on that dark place. But our fairy story moves in a radically different way. It's a young girl (and she's no Apollonian) who comes face-to-face with the Lindworm after he has eaten two previous brides-to-be. This particular girl is not a warrior for consciousness. Far from it. She's armed only with advice from her dead mother. And she was able to hear that advice only after she wept the night through on her mother's grave. Weeping and weeping through the night is a regular practice for those who hope to call a Divine presence that seems to be absent from their lives.

Though this girl is not Apollo, she's not Eve either, the first woman tempted by the snake in the Garden, the one who accepted the apple of knowledge from the snake and took a bite. Nor is she the Virgin Mary, who stayed perched with the serpent safely under her feet. She is the one who applies lye on the Lindworm's raw flesh and wears out brushes with all her strength, even as the snake lies skinless, shapeless, and lost. If ever there was a situation of "trust me, this is for your own good," this is it, but the scrubbing is not to clean the monstrous worm. Not at all. The girl knows the serpent can't live in the discarded, heartless, and angry way he has been. And she's brave. Brave enough to help him. The suggestion is that we all have enough bravery and compassion in us to face our own anger and heartlessness. We don't always think of ferocity and rough courage as part of a path of the heart, but this girl is certainly acting out of hope for the serpent's life and out of care for his radical possibilities. And she's as fierce as they come.

Already we can see that this story is a corrective to the heroic Apollonian fight for consciousness, but that doesn't mean it is a return to life in the Underworld. As with the frog in the Frog Prince story, the girl takes what is basically under earth and transforms it. We can even say she resurrects it. It is the feminine principle who takes this charge upon herself after she has agreed to marry the angry reptile. The serpent learns from the girl that she will not appear naked before him until he has removed his skins—one for one with her white shifts. He hopes to see the naked female (part of his own nature) at last. The shifts that cover her express a certain cleanness of spirit, almost a complement to the serpent's wild and sensuous earth-nature.

The recitation of the agonies of the serpent is excruciating. But we need to notice that its ordeal really has nothing to do with reforming its primitive nature, as we might imagine from the murky contrast with the girl's white dresses. Then what are they accomplishing during this strange ritual?

All the way back in very early Egypt, people worshipped the god Atum, a serpent known for bringing things to perfection. The Lindworm is that kind of serpent. And what will be brought to perfection here? The lively and glowing humanity, the hidden nature of this first Prince. His humanity is not going to be overly solar like his younger brother's. It will be more of a response to whisperings from the girl's mother, who is a full-time resident of the Underworld. And it will also be a response to the removal of the shifts, as his feminine soul—the Lindworm's and ours—is allowed to appear more and more clearly, one shift by one shift. His changes are a response to the hope of seeing the unadorned truth of the feminine. Some would say, because of the girl's alliance with the Lindworm, that she is part of the chthonic feminine, but that's a prejudice that doesn't apply to this story. The surprising element is that the painful work the girl and the serpent do together is an echo of the girl's earlier weeping. There's a call in it, as there is in the weeping and the scrubbing of the soul—this is the work of the attentive heart. It takes our full humanity to witness failure after failure in the face of the needs of those we love.

What is required from the Lindworm, and from us all, is reconciliation between the chthonic, dark, earthen world and the golden, light, airy one. But that is too simple. We have to notice that the reconciliation is accomplished with extreme, harsh, almost alchemical action on the earth-material of the serpent's body. And yet all of that ferocious scrubbing and shedding is done dispassionately.

The first two women who came to the Lindworm as prospective brides imagined a completion through him, and they got eaten for it. The third candidate knew he was a suffering being, and she imagined that the suffering being was not the same on the outside as it was on the inside. I can't tell you how much men appreciate that. And women, too. If someone else sees a rough exterior and knows it is a protection over wounds from past events, and also has faith in the beauty of the soul's interior, great healing is possible.

In this story, there's the amazing detail that the third bride has done all the work beforehand with her own shifts (which cover her heart area). She wears all of them at once for this project. She has clearly taken on some discipline involving the heart chakra. (In Indian thought, the centers of spiritual power in the human body, usually considered to be seven in number, are called chakras.) She isn't working in the power chakra, as the Lindworm did when he ate the first two brides; she is working with the heart.

For years, Rainer Maria Rilke's poetry came from his work in the heart area, and every giant snake that came to him he was able to deal with. That's the long labor of art. Kafka did all right, too. He lived with his mother and his sisters after his father died and worked in an insurance agency, which turned out to be a very responsible job, and he was marvelous at it. He helped people who were harmed in factories. What they had to do was so unpleasant and such dangerous work that many women threw themselves down stairs rather than continue with it. His care for their problems was extraordinary. Then, when he got home at six o'clock at night, he would have dinner with his mother and sisters and afterward go out with his male friends just to touch base and drink a little coffee and so on. Then he'd go back to his room, and at about eight thirty he'd stand in front of the window naked, breathing in cold air, which he was told by an American was a very good thing to do. Then he'd sit down to write. (I think he wrote *The Metamorphosis* in one night.) And then he'd get up at seven thirty the next morning and stagger off to work, dealing with accident problems, again tending to the heart.

Kafka tried to keep all of his life in one whole, and keep his sisters and his mother a part of it; and then when the others would sleep, he did the writing. What monsters did he not meet in the course of his life? His courage was amazing, and he did not feel superior to the problems he worked with.

The girl in this story has a lot of courage, too, and she doesn't blame the Lindworm for his exterior. Looked at with the perspective of inner development, the active soul here, armed with her brushes and lye, is requiring that the Lindworm see his own nature, clarify it, work with it, and learn to forgive those parts that need forgiveness. She can help him by reflecting honestly what she hears him saying. Even in a nation of individualistic sojourners, it is necessary to develop a real conscious awareness of how much self-forgiveness is required for this kind of work.

The Lindworm, as serpent, can also be associated with the spinal cord.

These days we want to live at the top of the head, in the brain, but for at least a couple of thousand years, a reptile has been representing the whole spine, and there's a part of each psyche that is at least a little bit reptilian. In this story, the ancient nervous system was thrown out with the first birth. The midwife tried to throw it out when she threw the little snake out the window. It wasn't considered necessary for civilized life. We used to say that the proper study of mankind is man, the whole man. But now we don't want to bother with the chthonic, the under-worldly energy as it lives in us. We'd rather see it projected on an entertainment screen. We'd rather meet people online, where there's no time for bodies. I heard a woman say on the radio that pretty soon, when our planet becomes uninhabitable, we'll have to emigrate to some other part of the universe, but most likely we won't be able to take our bodies along with us.

Throw out our older, more reptilian part, and our inner sister/brother gets very angry. It can't be ignored. And on the way to the wedding, in which of course the bride will wear a white dress and the groom will be dressed in black and white, you'll likely meet this older sibling again and you'll have to have your courage with you. The chthonic part has kept us going for millions of years; it has always been connected with our continued existence, that snake thing in there. It strikes and survives. Without that one, we'd have never gotten where we are.

We'd have died out.

Jung said, "Every part of us we do not love will regress and become more primitive." He didn't say, "Indulge it," or even, "Indulge in it." He said, "Accept that part," and he's right to say that. So if someone becomes a mathematician at twenty, and in order to be excellent in his field he gives up paying attention to his emotional body and doesn't think he needs it, it will regress, go backward in time, and become somewhat stubborn and violent. And it will happen that if he tries to recover his feeling body, he's less likely to be able to do it. If he sees this regression in another person, he'll say, "That thing is savage. I'm not dealing with it." Every part of you that you do not love will de-evolve.

I also like the way this story says you will not be married until you deal with the pain of that discarded and savage one. You can be married, all right. But it's not going to be a real marriage because, it seems, rejected siblings must be married first, and scrubbed until their honesty shines out. Only the third bride in this story knows how to honor the elder son. What we've most denied to the pained inner one is honor. The bride and the serpent have to be willing to scrub off a few layers of denial to get to its underlying humanity.

This third soul moves by repetition—of layers, of shifts, of scrubbings. As the psychologist James Hillman loved to point out, repetition is an excellent grounding for somebody with too airy a nature. Giving up novelty for practice helps a great deal with the necessary healing.

FOUR

THE DARK MAN

ONCE UPON A TIME THERE WAS A SOLDIER CALLED Hans who had just been discharged from his duties. While walking in the woods, in that curious sad mood we feel after something has ended, he met a Dark Man with an odd-shaped foot who asked him, "Why are you sad?"

"I don't know what to do next."

"You could work for me."

"What is the work?"

"You would live underground at my place and spend seven years in certain tasks. Then you're free. During that time, you won't be able to comb your hair, wash, cut your fingernails or your toenails or your beard, nor can you wipe the tears from your eyes."

So Hans went with the man, who took him underground and showed him three pots. "You'll be tending my three pots and keeping them boiling. You will not look into the pots. Is that clear? And you will sweep the shavings behind the door."

The soldier looked doubtful.

"Can you do it?"

"I can," Hans said.

He chopped wood, put the wood chunks under the huge, black, covered pots, kept the fires going, and swept the shavings behind the door. After three or four months, he said to himself, "I think I'll peek into one of these pots." He lifted the lid to the first pot and saw his sergeant sitting there.

"Oh ho!" he said to the sergeant. "You had me in your power, but now I have you in my power." And he added more wood to that fire.

He worked a few more months before he decided to peek into another pot. When he lifted the lid to the second pot, he saw his lieutenant sitting there. "Ah ha!" he said. "You once had me in your power, but now I have you in my power." And he added a lot more wood to that fire, too.

Six months later he couldn't resist his longing to peek into the third pot. He lifted the cover, and who did he see but his old general—General Gaweg—sitting there. "Well, well!" he said. "Once you had me in your power, but now I have you in my power." He chopped extra wood and added plenty of good dry oak under that pot.

When the Dark Man returned to see how the work was going, he remarked, "By the way, you looked into the pots, and if you hadn't added more wood, I really would have punished you."

Time seemed to pass faster now, what with the extra chopping each day.

Week by week the time went by, and the seven years were up.

The Dark Man returned and said, "You've done your work well." He swept up some of the shavings behind the door, put them into a gunnysack, gave the sack to the man, and said, "Here are your wages." The man was disappointed, but what can you do? Always remember to arrange your wages beforehand. The Dark One said: "When anyone asks you where you have come from, you say, 'From under the earth.' If they ask you who you are, you are to say, 'I am the Dark Man's Sooty Brother and my King as well.'" It didn't really make sense, but he memorized the sentence and prepared to go back to the world.

He left that workplace and the strangest thing was this: as he made his way up to our world, the shavings in his bag all turned to gold. That pleased him, of course. Eventually he came to an inn and asked for a room. "Where do you come from?" the innkeeper asked. "From under the earth." "Who are you?" "I am the Dark Man's Sooty Brother and my King as well." He hadn't shaved for seven years or wiped the tears from his eyes, so the innkeeper did not find him to be an appetizing guest. He said, "I'm sorry, but I have no rooms left for tonight." Then this worker made his first mistake—he opened the sack and showed the innkeeper his gold. The innkeeper said, "Well, as I think of it, I remember that my brother, who has been staying in Room Number Ten, is going away this weekend. You can have his room tonight." So it was. And in the middle of the night the innkeeper crept into the room and stole the gold. When our friend discovered it, he felt bad about it, but he said to himself, "It was through no fault of mine."

Then he decided to go back underground.

There he found the Dark Man and he told him what happened and what he wanted.

The Dark Man said, "Sit down. I'll wash you now and comb your hair, and cut your nails and beard, and wipe your eyes." When that was done, the Dark Man gave him a second bag of shavings and said, "Tell the innkeeper you want your gold back. If he doesn't do it, he'll have to come here and take your place. I will come for him." So Hans told that to the innkeeper and reminded him that if he went down, he would end up looking just like Hans did. That was enough; the innkeeper gave him the money back and more. So Hans was rich now.

He bought a coat of coarse cloth and started off to see his father, making a living as he went by making music on an instrument he had learned to play while he was underground. Eventually, the King of that country heard his music and was so taken by it that he offered

Hans his older daughter in marriage. When she saw the quality of his coat, she said, "I'd prefer to jump in the river." So he married the youngest daughter and got half the kingdom. When the King died, Hans inherited the entire kingdom for himself and his wife. That was good luck for him. As for the storytellers, we have to wander around with holes in our shoes.

* * *

Here Hans goes into the Underworld. There are many stories where to go into the Underworld is to go into an eclipse. When he's back from war, shadows thrown by the very earth we live on overwhelm him. The animals and the birds fall silent. Underground, his struggles will go on for years.

Hans is a Descender. It will be his job to keep three kettles boiling. For that he has to chop wood, but strangely, it is the shavings that turn out to be important. The Dark Man's instructions have been precise: *Sweep the shavings behind the door.* If we try that, we find that when we open the door to let our friends or enemies in, the shavings will not be visible. The opened door will hide them. But when the visitors leave and we close the door once more, we can see the shavings with our own eyes. So the story recommends a beautiful little dance of hiding and revealing. I've commented on this hiding in a book of mine called *Iron John*. There, a young man is urged to hide his gold; this man is to hide the shavings, before they become gold.

What are these shavings? We know that certain insights come only when we are depressed. If we go down in order to bring up a poem, let's say, certain lines will get written that tell us what we need to know and then they are thrown away. Therapy, too, when done well, produces many pre-thoughts and afterthoughts.

Certain ideas about life that we come upon in contemplation or while reading a great poem or novel might seem slim or too obvious for a while—but back in our regular life, these insignificant ideas turn to gold. The soldier from the story, when he is finally released from his service into the world, will have no choice but to ponder not only the horrors he has seen but how he must change his life now that he has seen them. That's good for him to think about.

And this chopping of wood one does when "underground"—what's the point of it? To keep the pots boiling, our story says. The fire tender finds, to his surprise, that his old sergeant, his lieutenant, and the general are each in a pot he has agreed to keep on the boil. These officers are some of the creatures inside his soul—and ours, too. The sergeant in the first pot is an image of authority. Some of us might glimpse a high school principal there, or a harsh parent, or the critic who offered humiliation when we showed our first poems. It used to be that we sat hunched up beneath those critics: inert, resigned, momentarily stuck. It is a great advance just to get them off our backs, into a pot, sitting in hot water, cooking.

Our story says that being passive toward these beings is not the thing. One has to be active. Boil them. That requires that we listen to our "Dark Man" in an "underground" place with some pots, a lot of chopping, heat, and ashes. And there's going to be soot. In other words, we explore our shadow and use all our faculties, both rational and feeling, our patience stretched to the extreme, to change the effect these inner commanding critics have in our lives.

The boiling requires active disobedience to the orders our first boss, the "commanding critic," gave us. To disobey his orders and to see the effect of that disobedience is to break the hold the critic has on us. But what is boiling like in daily life? Ask yourself hard questions. Learn the main influences in your father's life that are now affecting yours, learn which people shamed him in his childhood and how they did it, and, harder still, notice who places shame on you—that's one way of boiling. As adults it is our job to name the power we couldn't name that worked on us when we were children. That helps get rid of naïveté. In piling on wood to add heat to the fire, the soldier is encouraging his own insights. That's why the Dark Man won't punish him. When the young man looks in the pots and piles wood on the fire, he is doing just what needs to be done.

When Hans is about to go back up from the Underworld of the unconscious, the Dark Man warns him about the importance of language. When someone asks who he is, he is to say: "I am the Dark Man's Sooty Brother and my King as well." He is not to say, "I have spent six years getting my PhD in Brain Research, and six years teaching at the university, and I'm sure they'll give me tenure at the next faculty meeting" or "I am a young poet who has already gained a certain following for my work." Those would be naive answers that would call up inflation in the speaker and an urge to kill in the listeners. He is not to say, "I am the Dark Man's Shiny Brother" but "I am the Dark Man's Sooty Brother and my King as well." That phrase makes no more sense in German than in English, but it suggests that the process of cooking has freed him from some reliance on outer authority and that he is giving honor to darkness and shadow in learning to live his life. That's very good.

Alas, when the young man openly shows his bag of gold to the innkeeper, it is clear that he is still naive, even after the seven years of boiling. The complicated experiences he's had haven't cured his naïveté. That quality in young men hangs on. So I think we could profitably spend a little time talking about it.

"Naïveté," according to the dictionary, is "natural simplicity or artlessness, ingenuousness." But looked at from behind, it is a state of feeling that avoids the dark side of one's own motives or the motives of others. Naïveté discounts anger, fear, or greed and assumes more goodness in the world than perhaps there is. The naive person often refuses confrontation or combat, and, if thrown into combat by circumstance, often fails to notice that he has in fact been defeated. Wearing a white suit, he rides about the field where the defeat took place, waving to the onlookers with a smug look.

Naïveté was characteristic of American men around the middle and end of the last century, though realizations about the Vietnam War and the ugly effects of racism opened wounds that weren't going to heal without major changes. Then there was September 11, 2001. People understood immediately that fearmongering and lies had led the country into the Iraq War. With this realization, some naïveté fell away. Now, with social media and worldwide conversations on every imaginable topic, more people are likely to recognize other people's shadows and failures. Whether we can recognize our own is still in question.

The naive individual who refuses to notice the workings of his or her own shadow will never make the steps necessary to create a life of meaning. Unconscious acts, dazzling the innkeeper with our bag of gold, for instance, simply inflame him to more and more thievery. As I've said, naïveté works hand in hand with betrayal.

It takes concentration to notice the tricks of our own shadow. Let's say we forget to pay attention to inner work with authority figures or, in terms of the story, forget to add wood to the fire. We could slip into dependency and denial. For an artist with no place for the dark and ugly or, contrarily, with only a place for the dark and ugly, the work is kitsch in one way or the other. And everyone who sees it knows that the full emotional body is not present in it. At men's gatherings many complain that they grew up without any model of what an activated masculine emotional body is. They tell of robot-like fathers, playboys without depth, victims, fathers who won't defend themselves or their children when they're under attack. A man who is failing in this area might alternate between abusive behavior and a sheepish contrary softness. Robert Penn Warren said in the *Saturday Review* that the poem is a little myth of man's capacity for making life meaningful. And in the end the poem is a light by which we may see life.

* * *

Sometimes sons will try to activate their own emotional bodies through music or poetry or any of the other arts.

Practice of the arts alone doesn't necessarily succeed in opening the emotional body. A woman who notices that a man's emotional body is not activated will sometimes offer to help him express his feelings, or she might teach him to be more sensual. Though sex might deepen the integration of the physical and the emotional body for a woman, the same thing doesn't seem to work for a man; his early experience of sex is so different from hers, and not necessarily connected with the feeling body.

Instead, since the young man has a fantastic longing to find his place in the world, he needs to have help finding stories that describe aspects of life never mentioned in his family. This is why mentoring is so important. The old men in Australian aboriginal tribes, in New Guinea, and in Africa begin a complicated sequence of adventures, teachings, and trials with boys of the tribe in anticipation that they will learn enough to become men and not live their whole lives as children. They recite poems, act out myths, dance all night, and say outrageous things. An important feature of these ceremonies is the development of the connection with the earth and all its elements, so that the young men never forget that the earth is their home and gives birth to all things.

The story doesn't go into detail about how the emotional body is sustained after the seven years are up and the soldier returns to his life on the earth's surface. The False Innkeeper, the one in him and in us who prefers the ease of living out of habit and greed, has stolen his "insights." The old patterns have returned; apparently all his work has been for nothing. That's a state of diminishment we've all experienced. All the details in the story are fascinating. The response to the theft is not resignation, beer drinking, or more talks on male mythology, but acceptance of the need to "go back down" and this time say exactly what he wants and deserves.

At least this young Kettle Keeper, who tended the "fires of insight," has kept his promise not to cut his hair and nails or wipe his tears, and though he wants those things done, through a dangerous inertness in his emotional body, he fails to ask for what he wants. He is too agreeable, too helpful, or perhaps too ambitious for whatever project he has in mind. One could say he keeps on giving to those parts of the psyche that are insatiable. "Take no time for your humanity," he hears all day and night, "get on with my endeavor!" He might project his desires on the other characters in his drama—a wife, a boss, a son, a daughter, a guru—but he's really serving a part of himself that absorbs and absorbs and is never satisfied.

When the young man goes down the second time, he says to the Dark Man two things: "Give me more wages . . . cut my hair, trim my fingernails, wipe the tears from my eyes, and cut my toenails." I love this part; it seems to me so brilliant. Jung remarked, "American marriages are the saddest in all the world because the man does all his fighting at the office." Men live through years of a relationship secretly resentful, dimly enraged, passively hostile. And we are not talking only of marriage here or of other relationships in the outer world.

Suppose the Dark Man inside is waiting for an order. Some readers will remember Kafka's unparalleled story "Before the Law," about the doorkeeper and the suppliant. The suppliant sits by the door for months, for years, waiting for the moment when the door opens or when the doorkeeper falls asleep, or when he will be invited in. The years pass. Finally, when he's old and dying, he calls the doorkeeper over and whispers to him about the injustice of it all. The doorkeeper says, "Oh, this was your door; you could have gone through at any moment."

Passivity like that can weigh down any portion of a person's life—especially in the helpless disconnection from meaningful work. Many young people have seen themselves as functionaries only, whose job it is to slog along without dreams and only the mildest pleasure in what they do. They have adopted the belief that seems to be required of them: that they can never hope to live the life that best suits them. Now, however, the intricate connections among people all over the earth are encouraging both young and old to throw off emotional and mental stagnation. Then it happens that the mingling resentment, malice, and shame that is a natural response to living under despotic control is thrown off, too. No one knows what comes afterward.

We come now to a new understanding of the

meaning of the last phrase in the sentence: "I am the Dark Man's Sooty Brother *and my King as well.*" Evidence of kingship is the ability to say to the Dark Man in a convincing voice: "Cut my hair." He has come to the point where he will have to make up his own life. The inner King is the one in us to do this, to choose a good course for our life for the next six months, the next year, the next twenty years, without being overly contaminated by the ideas of others who think they know best. The story suggests we become our own Dark King (one including the shadow) and say, to ourselves in particular, what it is that we truly want.

What else can one say about this marvelous story?

We've found out that while the soldier was in the Underworld, he learned how to play music. He learned music through his emotional body. The poet Kabir mentioned several times hearing music coming from his own chest. When we learn how to play the musical instrument of our body, when the body itself makes music of its feeling, then a King's daughter hears it, or birds hear it, or other men hear it. That's when the man who left the tears in his eyes so he would remember his own grief, the Underworld worker, the citizen who now has to forge his own life, gains the entire kingdom for himself and for his bride. We should all be lucky enough to make that kind of music.

FIVE

ONE-TWO MAN

ONCE UPON A TIME THERE WAS A BOY WHO WAS living with his grandmother, the father having died some years before, and his mother seemingly gone, perhaps living somewhere else. His grandmother, with whom he got along well, was raising him. But one early summer day when he was about fourteen, he said to his grandmother, "There's absolutely nothing to do around here. I'm bored." His grandmother replied, "Why not go out into the fields and dig some roots. Then we won't be hungry in the winter." The boy thought this was a good idea, and he soon began to enjoy it. He would leave every morning with his digging stick, and after a while he could guess where a big root was likely to be. Moreover, he discovered other roots he had never eaten before. Each evening, he'd add his new roots to the pile he had already gathered, and these roots were the first things he'd look at in the morning.

Early one fall day, he got up, went out to look at the pile, and came running back. "All the roots are gone, Grandma," he cried, and he wept. His grandmother replied, "The spirit of your father came last night and took away the roots. That means he wants to get in touch with you. If you sit down, I'll tell you a story that I've never told you because I thought you were not quite old enough. It's the story of Stone Shirt.

"There was once a man who became a very powerful shaman and magician, but he used those gifts for his own gain; then he began to harm people. When he understood that people were angry at him, he made a stone shirt for himself that covered his whole heart and chest area, so that arrows and spears bounced off. People called him Stone Shirt.

"Stone Shirt is the one who killed your father. He wanted to have your mother; and after he took her away, he tried to kill you also, but something happened, so his plan didn't work. The story tells you why your mother is not living with you. Stone Shirt is keeping her in his wigwam. That's how it happens that you are living with me. Tomorrow morning, I want you to walk to that oak tree over there and dig underneath it. You'll find your father's bones buried under its roots."

So the boy dug there, and several feet down he found his father's bones. He lifted them carefully, brought them up, and put them on the grass. Right away he fell into a deep sleep. He slept for three days while the spirit of his father taught him all the things the father would have taught the boy if he were still alive—how to trail deer, how to find bear, how to know what sort of weather is coming, how to know where you are in the forest, how to sleep in the snow, as well as the names of certain rocks and trees. Then he taught the boy what it meant to be a warrior and what a warrior did and what he thought and how he walked. The father taught his son these things for three days and the boy listened well.

Then, as the dream came to an end, he said to the boy, "I want you to go back to where my bones were buried. Dig down beneath and you'll find the stone ax my father gave to me, his father gave to him, and his grandfather gave to his father. They were from the Crane Clan, known for bringing peace when there were quarrels. The stone ax belongs to the fathers. Take this ax home and tell your grandmother to hit you on the skull with it. She should split you in two all the way down the middle."

The boy dug farther down under the oak and found the stone ax. When he returned to the house and told his grandmother to hit him with it, she refused. "I love you too much for that. Such a blow would kill you. Please don't ask me again."

The boy then told her that this request had come from his father's spirit. At last, she agreed to it. She took up the ax, steadied herself, and split him all the way to the ground. After that day, the boy was known as One-Two Man because he was no longer one man but two who were just alike.

One-Two Man now spoke their first sentence: "I'm going to find Stone Shirt's cave and bring back my mother." He understood he needed some help for that and so he went to the forest. During all the years he was growing up, he played in the forest alone, and he had made friends with a Snake, a Mouse, a Coyote, a Wolf, and a Bighorn Sheep. Now he went to consult them. They said, "Don't try it. It's too hard. No arrow or spear can pierce the stone shirt, and besides, he has a guard at his teepee. There's a gazelle that guards the entrance. It has an eye on the end of every hair. Besides that, Stone Shirt has two daughters by an earlier marriage. They are expert at arrows and never miss. We think it's best if you let the whole thing go and just forget about it." One-Two Man said he planned to go ahead anyway, and so the creatures all agreed to help. That's the way that went.

The Bighorn Sheep brought his gift first, which was a horn of water that would never go empty, very valuable in such dry country. One-Two Man accepted that gift. The Bighorn Sheep went back to his place. Meanwhile, the others—the Snake, the Mouse, the Coyote, and the Wolf—would help plan the attack, which would have to proceed very carefully.

All five of them, or really all six of them, since One-Two Man was now two, traveled toward Stone Shirt's cave and made camp a mile or two away. They began planning the attack. Coyote and Wolf went on for hours. They talked over and over again about the gazelle with one eye at the end of each hair, how to deal with that, how many eyes it had, whether any of the eyes close during the day, and so on. They discussed the plans that people had made earlier in similar situations. They debated various strategies for weeks. The Mouse got to hating these discussions and the Snake was at his wit's end; he couldn't take it anymore. So one night while the Coyote and the Wolf were still arguing their strategies after midnight, the Snake slipped away, stung the gazelle to death, and returned. When he reported this in the morning, the Wolf and the Coyote got into a disagreement about which of them had put the idea into the Snake's head. They argued for many hours about it.

When that was over, they began discussing the second problem, which was what to do with the two daughters. They were Stone Shirt's daughters and very tough. When they slept, there were strong bows beside them and those bows were always strung. The daughters were excellent markswomen and could hit a mark even at a great distance. These two women would have to be approached with great care.

Coyote and Wolf made up and threw away many ingenious ideas. They talked for days, for a week, for three weeks. Mouse finally had had enough, crawled near the bows on the ground, and gnawed until each string was almost severed. The instant one put pressure on the string it would snap. Mouse, when he returned, told everyone what he had done, and Coyote and Wolf got into a long argument over which one of them had dropped the hint that led to this solution; and a lot of talk went into the air that way. Finally, One-Two Man felt that the time had come.

One-Two Man saw his mother out walking near the river and he managed to convey to her what they were going to do. Then he told her to stand with her back to the teepee and look out over the river while they did it. Meanwhile, Coyote and Wolf argued what to do about Stone Shirt himself, who had such marvelous protection against all weapons and arrows. This talk went on and on, day after day. Brave Wolf and wily Coyote kept arguing about the best way to proceed.

Meanwhile, Snake had noticed that Stone Shirt went out early in the morning to answer the call of nature, and so Snake went to that place, waited underneath a big leaf before dawn, and stung him in the ass and killed him. That was the end of Stone Shirt! After that, what was left to do? All six of them went to Stone Shirt's teepee together. One-Two Man rescued his mother, and everyone felt very good about the success of the effort. One-Two Man thanked all of the animals. The Snake, the Mouse, the Wolf, and the Coyote returned to the forest. That's how One-Two Man did it all; he achieved what neither his grandmother nor the animals thought he could do, and by that effort he finished all the work that his father hadn't been able to do. That's how the story came to me. That's how it ran and runs now, and I'm sending it back to the forest and to the place where it still lives.

* * *

As the story begins, the young boy lives alone with his grandmother and he has given her his love. When she suggests that he dig roots, he does that. It gets him out of his boredom and out of the house. Simultaneously, it allows him to see that there are precious discoveries to be made below the surface of life, and he soon develops the ability to recognize signs telling him where these precious things will appear. He is beginning to enjoy his work, to be good at it. He is happy to help the family, especially with the accumulation of this food. A digging task can be quite valuable.

Then one day his pile of roots is gone. His grandma says his dead father wants to contact him, so he will have to be done with accumulation and with digging. The boy is at an age of initiation, when a father can enter a boy's emotional world in a new way. The boy will learn some important things from his male ancestors.

The grandmother is not wary of contact from the father, even though he abides in another world. Her heart is open to other wisdom besides her own. She knows that the boy's father was killed by Stone Shirt, who has a fierce hostility to growth and warmth, and stays removed from ordinary people. Women suffer because of Stone Shirt's coldness, which is unlike the coldness of the witch of most fairy stories, whose wild greed puts her in contact with humans. Her endless desiring can be somehow endearing; she wants what she wants and someone must give it to her. But Stone Shirt's way is alienating. He steals feeling from the human community and takes it far away.

Stone Shirt has captured the feeling of the young male in this story. Most likely the feeling problem goes way back in the family's history, and many forces will be needed to help get the feeling back. Even the creatures will be called on to bring their own species of wisdom. The boy's father can't be much help, except from the other world, where the story takes for granted that he is in touch with the teachings of many generations.

The family problem seems to have been a repression of feeling. The grandmother reveals to the boy that it is because of Stone Shirt that his mother is living far from him. At the same time that he learns this, he learns that there is covetousness and murder in the world. She instructs the boy to find his father's bones under the roots of a tree. When he finds them, he falls into a deep sleep, and there his father teaches him many things that will help him to live in the world. Then the father says, "Dig down beneath my bones and find the stone ax my father gave to me, his father to him, his father's father to him, and so on far back into the lineage," perhaps as far back as the Neolithic stone ax, millennia ago. The boy finds the ax and tells his grandmother she is to use it to split him in two. She is reluctant, but he convinces her. The old fathers want the boy to have two different ways of knowing. They are to be separated, given different names.

As soon as he is split, he says, "I'm going to find Stone Shirt's cave and bring back my mother." In the midst of his learning about the world, by rescuing his mother he will become the defender of the male mode of feeling for the whole family. He will be in great danger; even his wild side is not equipped for that much danger. He will need help from sources he hasn't yet encountered. We could say that the moon side—the moving, changing, ephemeral moon side—has to be split from the vigorous, unchanging consciousness belonging to the sun side. We know that as soon as the boy is split, there is going to be a reflective witness in him.

The split helps the boy see that a river has more than one source, the dawn has more than one morning, gods existed before monotheism, fire burns with more than one stick, and forest ecology has no one species dominant through all time. There is a time to know oneself as two beings, one on each side of the ax.

The man who has seen and recognized the split would not identify himself with one of the two sides. He would wonder, with each work of art he meets, whether it talks to both sides of himself—to the secretive moon side as well as the confident sun side. (I identified for years with my sun side. It seemed the right thing to do.)

I sense that the side of the male mode of feeling, if that is what the boy is learning about, has a strong component of longing—for what, we don't know, but I think it has to do with something the German mystic Angelus Silesius said:

> *If you could turn your heart into a cow stall, Christ would be born again on earth!*

The boy sets out to ask the animals to help him get his mother back. These animals are not so clearly instinctual as they might be in another story. They seem to be a version of the different ways people behave in the world he'll enter as a man; but as animals, they are still innocent. Since this is a Native American story, the animals are also wise. We have to assume that they have contact with the eternal. He has known them from a lost, innocent time when he played together with them. He tells the animals he wants to kill Stone Shirt. They wisely say, "Don't try it."

We need to look briefly at the five beings, creatures, or faculties the boy meets in the forest. Two of the animals, the Mouse and the Snake, are hiding, retiring, secretive, introverted, nonverbal, private ground-huggers. Coyote is a talkative, pushy, aggressive, extroverted, public, and exhibitionistic ground-runner, while Wolf, another ground-runner, is isolated and wintry. The fifth, the Bighorn Sheep, is a mountain type. He likes heights. He is fierce in battles in spring, yet he possesses a reserve of calm. His gift is a horn of water that never runs dry. When he has given that, he returns to the mountains. I connect him with a fundamental courage that is sufficient for movement into the unknown. The mountain sheep inside us drives forward and gives us libido enough for our whole lives. A man finds this energy when he has been split by the father's ax. That's what the story says.

The Mouse is quite different. He belongs, along with the rats and squirrels, to the company of "gnawers," whose master, "the Rat-Wife," Ibsen describes in *Little Eyolf*. She can call the gnawers away from an island and, let's say, into the sea and drown them. But it is not clear if we should get rid of all the gnawers. Certain things gnaw at us, and they exist at some sort of threshold between the conscious life and the unconscious life, so they can slip back down in a moment and be gone. They have almost no defense but hiding, and yet, when something is strung too tightly in us so that it's impossible for us to unstring it, and it is dangerous to cut it with a knife, the gnawers do the work. The gnawers take fifteen years over a decision that we don't have the clarity to solve quickly. The gnawers leave annoying nests in the backs of drawers and occasionally make their nests using the edges of our diaries or the centers of diplomas and real estate deeds; moreover, the fierce smell of their nests penetrates our nostrils whenever we open one of those drawers. But, at last in gratitude, one day we are gnawed free from what has bound us and we say: Blessed be the gnawers that chewed through the string of that bow.

The Snake is something else again. Snakes, too, as the story suggests, dislike a lot of verbiage; they withdraw, they hide, and yet they do not lose touch with the aim of it all. After all the meetings and discussions between the characters of this story, it is Snake that cuts through the talk and bites Stone Shirt on the ass and kills him. Does that suggest that after the boy spends so much time listening to others, he will strike out and kill his enemy just to wipe him off the map? Not so. The instincts are still alive in the interior world, too. And after the boy has seen his problem from the different angles the animals represent, he has to do something about it. He has to act. He has the courage of the Wolf to advise him, so he won't be scared that what has happened once will happen always. He has the cunning of Coyote, so he can go around his own fears and the paralysis of his anger. And, like the Snake, he won't take an elevated approach. He doesn't have to stay on a higher plane.

This isn't a hero's story. It is a story about the

development of consciousness. The father insists on it. From off in the other world he takes the first step; then the grandmother tells the story of the father's death, and she's the one who splits the boy in two. Something innate in the boy, something given at birth, has allowed him to recognize a helpful spirit in each of the different animals. Now the differences among them are clearer, and he spends a lot of time talking and listening and learning what they have to say so he can plan what to do. These are a series of acts of consciousness. He listens and listens, and though the animals don't act together, as he'd expected, they cooperate in their own ways; and the work that needs to get done is done.

Snakes are royalty, as D. H. Lawrence noticed when he met a snake at a drinking trough, but quirkily obedient to his fears and to Christian snake-hatred, he threw a stick at it anyway:

> For he seemed to me again like a king,
> Like a king in exile, uncrowned in the underworld,
> Now due to be crowned again.

And so, I missed my chance with one of the lords
Of life.
And I have something to expiate:
A pettiness.

The ancients guessed that because the Snake sheds his skin every year, he knows more about how to grow and how to avoid stagnation and how to refuse automatic patterns than the other creatures know. The Gnostics associated the Snake with the spinal cord, and this detail reminds us that the spinal intelligence, though physically below the brain, can intervene decisively if necessary. Here, the Snake is Lord of the Underworld. He makes his home in places lower than we go, and one would be foolish to embark on a deadly task without his decisiveness.

* * *

As we know, Stone Shirt has enclosed his heart and lungs in stone. The psychic arrows of shamans who might wish to harm him can't penetrate the stone. And he has a gazelle Guardian—and each of its hairs has an eye on the end of it. The gazelle is famous for watch-fulness and for swift reflexes in danger, so the story says that the psyche of the one who killed the boy's father is extremely alert. Our human consciousness does not know how to deal with that alertness. The effort to kill Stone Shirt could end right there.

The boy and the animals have arguments, discussions, proposals, tangents, and they have a good time together. All their talk expresses their inability to deal with the invisible, or with that which becomes translucent or transparent to the light. For ages, human beings have imagined the eye with light coming out of it rather than going into it. The gazelle with all the eyes then would be virtually invisible or transparent from all the light. One day, the Snake gets tired of all the babble, slips out, and stings the one they all fear. In psychic terms, the spinal cord can put anything outside the reach of ordinary consciousness. Even our defensiveness can't resist it; it can pull our alertness into oblivion. Neruda says:

> *If you ask where I come from I have to start talking with broken*
> *objects,*

with kitchenware that has too much bitterness,
with animals quite often rotten,
and with my heavy soul.

What have met and crossed are not memories,
nor the yellow pigeon that sleeps in forgetfulness.

But even when oblivion has eaten the gazelle Guardian, Stone Shirt is still well guarded, for his two "daughters" own bows that are always strung, and the daughters shoot very well. If a male, aiming to reverse his father's fate and keep his own soul alive, tries to move into the force field in which our young man's father died, he will find a feminine power. That kind of feminine power is hostile to One-Two Man. It guards the father's murderer instead. That is very strange, and yet it reminds us of the hostile psychic energy that many ancient cultures identified. It is as if Stone Shirt gives an approval to his daughters that allows the death of a young man's soul, even if it ends all possibility for his true humanity.

The Wolf and the Coyote don't know how to defeat that force field, and that is not surprising, because each is rather advanced in evolution and each has evaded nature's conservative power sometime in the far past. Both Coyote and Wolf are highly intelligent, curious about all unusual sights and objects, devoted warmly to their families, good explorers of the earth's surface, and capable of admiring human beings.

They differ also in many ways. The American Indians talk of a trickster embodied in Coyote. This trickster possesses unpredictability, which shows itself in juvenile pranks rather than sober judgments, in riddle mentality rather than the doctrinal, in ingenious escapes rather than resigned imprisonment, and in a love of all things low and outrageous rather than a longing for the higher consciousness. He farts to settle a question instead of appealing to higher principle. But he is not earthbound. He loves air, mentality, mental fight, intellectual playfulness, and good jokes.

The Wolf is something quite different. American Indians associated the Wolf with clear-eyed will and solitary, disciplined living. He holds darkness, winter, night, and unexpected destructiveness, but he can be tamed to a degree. He is far along on the evolutionary path. He is a good model for human intelligence in many ways, and when he and Coyote argue for days and weeks, they do represent some human way of approaching difficult problems. Wolf and Coyote lay out all contingencies to embrace the problem of the Hostile Daughters and their Two Strung Bows. They waste time, force time to pass, ignore body wisdom, forget to worship silence, forget to wait for the right moment. Instead, they fill the cave with excitable words, they stimulate the shallow, verbal part of the psyche, drink caffeinated beverages, eat chocolate, stay up late, call each other names, invent absurd schemes, and claim credit for everything good that has happened, up to and including Creation. Without all the babble, the Mouse and Snake in us will not do their work. We have to heat up the psyche, and this is something frequently forgotten by men and women who abruptly leave a university town to settle down alone in a bog. A man alone, a woman alone, or a man and wife together can live off the capital invested by Wolf and Coyote in their graduate school days for a while, but eventually the psyche cools down, and then no inner work gets done at all, though their lives now have a purity and wholesomeness lacking in the city.

In the story, Mouse, driven in exasperation out of

his habitual and complacent nervousness, gets so heated that he slips out one night, runs all the way to the cave, and gnaws the two bowstrings nearly through, silently, in a way that doesn't disturb the sleep of the objects.

* * *

When Mouse gets home and reports this, the rest of the psyche feels much better. That doesn't prevent Wolf and Coyote from engaging in a ferocious verbal battle on the question of which of them had inspired the Mouse. At last they settle down to discuss the most effective way of penetrating the stone shirt, and they manage to do that for several weeks, no doubt discussing huge iron javelins, thousand-degree ovens that would burn up Stone Shirt and his vest, microbe colonies that might get under the shirt and cause inflammation so that Stone Shirt would have to remove it, and so on. They had a lot of fun, but it wasn't fun for the Snake. It knew that the spinal cord goes all the way down to the ass, and that's where the snake stung Stone Shirt as he was relieving himself, during what was probably his only human moment that day.

Somewhere along the way, One-Two Man, meeting

his mother while she is out walking, tells her that when the final action starts, she should not take part, or even watch, but look out over the lake. Looking out over the lake, she will have her face toward eternity, and when our mother's face is toward eternity, we can fight more freely.

* * *

Stone Shirt is male. He carries a hard shell around the heart area. (I sensed that shell around my father's heart area and sense it around my own.) Maybe we see our fathers killed every day. Aren't we all afraid of being killed? Sometimes we can watch a so-called meek man hesitate and finally give no opinion; and we can say he is afraid of being wrong; that may be, but he might also be afraid of being killed. We're in complicated material here.

Stone Shirt confuses his desire for feeling with love for his captive, which caused him to steal the young man's feeling as well. And something needs to be done about him, something in the male world. We need to sleep for three days on our father's bones, however uncomfortable they may be underneath us. We need to find our father's ax and ask our grandmother to split us down the middle. She doesn't want to do it; she represents unity. And if it is painful, we choose it anyway. Rumi speaks in favor of an open feeling around pain, and of not intellectualizing it:

> *A person hit a Worker a good strong blow from behind.*
> *The Worker swung around to return it; and the man said:*
> *"Before you hit me, I have a question for you.*
> *Now this is it: that sound: was it made by my hand or your*
> *   neck?"*
> *"The pain I am feeling does not give me leave for speculation.*
> *These things are all right to worry about if you are feeling no pain."*

In the urgency of removing power from the feeling life, it is probably wise to remain split for a longer period than our integrative culture tells us to. One part of us is educated and one is not, particularly the feeling side, for men. I want to write poems for each side that both parts can understand. I don't want to leave one or the other isolated, unloved, disdained, and uncared for.

* * *

Could we say that a woman's instinct is to heal wounds and a man's to make them larger, to take on the painful tension of what has been left undone, what was never given, what was given that was never acknowledged, the thefts we've endured, the inheritance from family? No metaphor will do. At the end of the story we know that in trying to become a good man, we can close up our wounds too soon, allowing Stone Shirt to hold feeling prisoner in his cave. It is part of our work to free her.

SIX

THE WHITE BEAR
KING VALEMON

A YOUNG GIRL GOES OUT IN THE FOREST ONE DAY AND sees a White Bear playing with a golden wreath. He is lying on his back, balancing the wreath in his paws. The girl is drawn to gold and so she likes the wreath better than anything she has ever seen. The bear tells her she can have the golden wreath if she marries him.

The youngest daughter—offspring of royalty—hurries home and tells her father all about the adventure that she has had in the forest with the White Bear and his golden wreath. Like most fathers, the King is glad that his daughter has become interested in spiritual gold, but he is unwilling that she should marry a White Bear just to get it. So he tries various worldly tricks to keep her at home. A golden wreath is not that hard to get, so he speaks earnestly to the goldsmiths and asks them to make a wreath of the sort she has described. After some days of labor, the goldsmiths produce a wreath. The daughter says, "No, no. It was oval, not round." So the goldsmiths go back to work and make a new wreath, and the daughter says, "No, the leaves were longer and thinner. They're not willow-shaped, either." So this process takes a long time. Sooner or later the father has to recognize that the heavenly wreath was not made by human hands. As human beings, our problem is how to get the golden wreath without paying a lot for it. But the daughter in us will not accept any halfway wreaths. She wants the real one, and she will have to marry the White Bear to get it.

The father thinks to himself, "The eyesight of bears is not very good. A bear couldn't tell one of my daughters from another. By rights, my oldest daughter should be married first, so I'll have a wedding dress made for her, and when the White Bear arrives, she will walk out to meet him. To a bear, one daughter is the same as another."

So the White Bear tells the King he will come for his bride next Thursday. Next Thor's Day? Thor, the god of thunder and lightning. That will be a good day. "It will turn out well," the White Bear thinks. "Thor's Day is the day for wild things. Wednesday—Odin's Day—would not be so good. Odin is a kind of intellectual, a bit quarrelsome. Thor's Day is better."

Making ready for the White Bear's arrival, the King has enlisted a few ne'er-do-wells, some out-of-work farmers, some one-armed carpenters, several barflies. He has given all of them weapons and placed them before the gates of the castle.

At about ten in the morning, when the White Bear arrived, the weapons the men had didn't seem to work and the White Bear knocked them all down and entered the castle. He said, "Well, well. Is my sweet bride somewhere around here?"

The King led out his oldest daughter. She wasn't much to look at, but he had put a veil over her head. The White Bear said, "Climb on my back." She did this, and he set off for his own castle, which was a few miles away. He took a cross-country route through the pine-woods. She had to hold on to his fur, but his back was broad and the fur deep. After a while he said to her: "My dear, have you ever sat more softly than you are sitting now?" The oldest daughter said, "On my father's lap, I did sit more softly than I'm sitting now." After a bit he said, "Have you ever seen more clearly than you're seeing now?" She said, "From my father's castle I saw more clearly than I'm seeing now."

"Oh no!" the White Bear said. "This is the wrong one." And he threw her off his back and kept on going. So the oldest daughter had to get home on her own. The thornbushes and hemlock branches pulled at her clothes, and when she got home, hours and hours later, she was a mess. No one could have recognized her dress as a bridal dress.

On the next Thor's Day, everyone figured the White Bear would show himself once more, and he did. This time the King had the second daughter ready to go; the seamstresses had worked up a new bridal dress, with a fairly thick veil, and the whole process started again. This time, the King brought in some soldiers from a neighboring regiment; he told them to dig rifle pits, and he even had a few cannons left over from the most recent war with Sweden.

By ten a.m. everything was ready, and sure enough, the White Bear arrived.

When he saw the rifles and guns aimed at him, he stood on his hind legs, gave a roar, and rushed in. Somehow, none of the bullets hit him. The cannon misfired, knocking over its own crew, and the battle-hardened soldiers threw away their muskets and headed for the south. The White Bear King walked into the castle grounds and said quietly to the King, "Is my bride somewhere nearby?"

Out came the second sister. "What a beautiful gown!" said the White Bear. She said her good-byes to her father and others, climbed onto the White Bear, and off they went. It wasn't easy holding on; the White Bear definitely had somewhere to get to, and he rushed through the forest at a good pace. But he had a broad back. An hour or so later, the White Bear turned his head toward her. "Have you ever sat more softly than you're sitting now?" "Oh yes," she said, "at times when I sat on my father's lap, I was sitting more softly than

I am sitting now." After a bit, the White Bear asked, "Have you ever *seen* more clearly than you're seeing now?" "Oh yes," she said, "when I went with my father to his look-out on top of the castle, I did see more clearly than I'm seeing now."

"Bad news!" he said. "It's the wrong one!" And the White Bear threw her off and rushed away. There she was, all alone in the woods, with prickly bushes and pieces of bark pulling at her bridal gown. It wasn't long before she looked a mess. She did find her way home finally. The King and his servants did the best they could to fix her up, but she was not happy about what had happened.

The King spent the next week sending private messengers to Kings nearby, reminding them of favors in the past. From the neighboring Kings, he managed to get forty or so soldiers, as well as some specialists and out-of-work generals. They set up some pointed sticks. At ten o'clock on Thor's Day they were all ready. The White Bear came loping along; no one could remember exactly what happened, but the soldiers got confused and went into battle with no shells in their guns, and the sharpshooters fell out of the trees; it was chaos. When the smoke cleared, the White Bear King was already inside the castle grounds, where he inquired politely, "I wonder if my dear bride is nearby."

Now the youngest daughter came out of the castle, beautifully dressed in an old-fashioned wedding dress. The Queen's maidservants all looked sad and adjusted the daughter's gown. The King said a reluctant farewell. She climbed on the White Bear King Valemon's back, and they were off.

The White Bear, going at a fast clip, turned his head after a few miles and asked, "Have you ever sat more softly than you're sitting now?" The bride said, "Never." After a while, he asked, "Have you ever seen more clearly than you're seeing now?" "Never!" she said. "Ah, she's the right one," the White Bear said, and they kept going.

After a while they arrived at a castle, which was the home of the White Bear King. In that castle there was much elegance and abundance. Tall candles lit a table, and the Princess and the White Bear King dined together. He escorted her to the bedroom, which was very dark. But once they were both in bed, she would discover that he indeed had strong arms—and she was in bed with a man, and not a bear.

The Princess was lonesome sometimes in the castle during the day, but she looked forward to the night, which always went by in a sweet and affectionate way. After several months of this sort of life, she wasn't surprised when she found herself with child. She prepared herself to give birth, and all of that went well. But the strange thing was that the baby disappeared soon after. No one could explain it. The baby was simply gone the morning after it was born. In the next two years, two other babies were born, and they both vanished in the same way.

So many strange things happened that the disappearance of the babies seemed to be just one thing more. But she was lonely, so one day she said, "I would like to go home and see my mother and father." The White Bear King thought this was a good idea, and he said: "Trust what your father says, but you should be suspicious of your mother's advice."

She did go home, and the homecoming was sweet. Of course, her sisters were very curious about how the

White Bear King was as a husband. They had many questions. "Does he wash his paws every day? How do you deal with supper? Does he leave hair all over the floor? You need to have a look at him. Does he have very sharp teeth? You'd better find out what he's really like or he might eat you up." The sisters' suspicions are not surprising. We know that each of us has greedy beings inside that are jealous. And we have fathers and mothers whose advice is often dubious and sometimes leads to suffering.

The mother and father could overhear the sisters' conversation. "I think you should let things be as they are," the father said to his youngest daughter. But the mother said, "Take this candle back with you. One night, after he has fallen asleep, light the candle and hold it up. Then you'll know one way or the other who you are married to. That's my advice."

The Princess brought the candle back to the Bear King's castle. The first night home they made love, and when her lover fell asleep, the Princess got up, quietly lit the candle, and held it up in the dark room. She looked first at his feet; they were large and shapely and seemed beautiful to her. His shins and knees were elegant. She moved the light over his thighs; they were strong and well-shaped, and other things in that neighborhood were handsome and fine. She found his stomach firm and his chest broad. He was without a doubt a lovely man; and now that she had seen his strong body, she was even more curious about his face. However, as she lifted the candle this time, one drop of hot wax fell on his shoulder and woke him up.

"Oh, my dear one! Why did you do that?" he cried. "If only you had waited another month, I could have been a human being both night and day! Now I can no longer stay here." He turned into a bear and rushed out the door.

She cried out, "Don't go!"

"Now I cannot stay," he answered.

He rushed on all fours out of the castle and into the forest, and she ran after him. She tried to hold on to his fur, but the underbrush and branches tore at her, and she fell. The White Bear King rushed on ahead and the Princess was on the forest floor alone. She wandered around for a long time without shelter or food. If she met a person, she would ask about the White Bear King Valemon. The answer was always the same: "I've never heard of him." After a long time, she saw a hut. When she knocked, the door opened. A woman lived there with a small girl. She was glad to talk with the woman. When she'd received some food, she got down on the floor and played with the little girl and asked her many questions about dollhouses and crickets.

Later, when she was about to leave, the little girl was sad. "Mother, she's been so good to us. Could we give her the scissors?" The old woman said, "If you want to." The scissors were special. Whenever the scissors were opened and closed, cloth appeared on its own. You could have any cloth you wanted: Indian silks, Irish linen, French lace, Danish flannel, and so on. The visitor was delighted to have the scissors. As she left the house, she said to the woman, "Might I inquire if you have seen the White Bear King Valemon?"

The woman said, "Yes, I have, as a matter of fact. He came past here about a month ago. He was traveling very fast—heading west."

The Princess was glad to hear that news. She walked farther west through the forest, and a few days later she saw a second hut. Amazingly, it, too, was inhabited by a small girl and a woman. The woman served the traveler tea, as is only right, and shared the tea with the daughter, and the traveler asked her questions like, "Have you learned the alphabet yet? What stories do you know? Do you go to school? Do you have any friends in the woods?" This went on for quite a while. When she was about to leave, the daughter said, "Mother, she has been so good to us. Could we give her the flask?"

Now this flask was a remarkable flask—when you took off the cover and turned it, any liquid that one desired poured out. If you thought "cognac," cognac came, or espresso came, or wine, or jasmine tea or chai or Persian liqueurs. "If you want to give her the flask, it's okay," the mother said. The small girl was so glad to give it to the visitor. After the visitor had thanked her hosts, she turned to the woman and asked, "May I ask if you've seen the White Bear King Valemon go by here?"

The mother answered, "I have. He came by here about a week ago. He was going very fast toward the west. I'm not sure you can catch up with him." So the Princess walked faster now. After a while she happened on a third hut in which a woman lived with a young girl. Once more tea; once more the visitor paid much attention to the child. She helped her make little dolls out of pinecones and rags and asked her many questions. "Which animal would you be?" When the visitor was about to leave, the girl said, "Mother, she has been so good to us. Could we give her the tablecloth?"

This tablecloth was magic, too. Each time you spread it out on a table, food appeared on its own: roast duck, salmon, sweet-and-sour soup, lamb stew, potato cakes, chocolate mousse. Any dish that you thought of appeared. The woman said, "If you want to give her the tablecloth, that's good." As the visitor was about to go, she turned to the woman and said, "By the way, do you know where the White Bear King Valemon is now?" The mother replied, "I do! He came by here about three days ago, going west. I heard he's on his way to the Glass Mountain."

So the Princess hurried toward the Glass Mountain. After several days, she saw it looming over the trees. As she approached its base, she noticed the ground was covered with the bones of all the men and women who had tried to climb it and failed. The glassy sides were steep, and there were no footholds.

She noticed another hut nearby. When she knocked at the door and was invited in, she realized that it was different in several ways from the previous huts she had visited. A middle-aged woman, not young, not old, lived there with four young children. There was evidence of a man's tools. The Princess saw no food anywhere; the family was obviously starving. Everyone's clothes were tattered. Soon the children confided in her. "Lots of times we have no food. Mother tells us the stones are apples, and it does make the soup taste better."

It didn't take long for the Princess to open the table-cloth and spread it out.

Roast lamb, good cheese, and fresh vegetables appeared. The mother and the children ate and ate. And the flask poured orange juice and milk and hot cider. The visitor now took out the scissors and snipped out cloth for dresses, winter coats, woolen trousers, winter underwear, shawls, and socks. When supper was over, the tablecloth provided some salt beef, dried cod, goat cheese, and other things that would last the winter. When everyone had been provided for, the visitor turned to the mother and asked, "What has happened with the White Bear King Valemon?"

The woman looked at her awhile and said, "Are you the one? Are you the beloved who lifted the candle?" The visitor said yes, she was that one. She told how she had been searching for weeks and had walked a long time.

"Well," the mother said, "the White Bear King is up on the mountain right over there; he is going to be married in three days."

The Princess was shocked. "To whom?"

"Her," the mother replied.

"What do you mean, Her?"

"Her. The Great One. She lives on top of the Glass Mountain, and she has a great appetite. Fat dogs tend to disappear when they get near her. She's been known to eat a hundred roasted songbirds at one sitting. Skeleton hands serve her tea and footlong warts grow out of her nose. Many animals do whatever she wants. The wedding is in three days."

The visitor thanked the woman and started out to climb the Glass Mountain.

But it was slippery. She could get no hold. She slipped and fell off its side again and again. The mother whose table she had heaped with food came out and said: "This isn't going to work. I am grateful to you for feeding and clothing the children. Nothing could have been more wonderful. My husband is coming back tonight. He's a blacksmith. I'll ask him to make some iron claws for your hands and feet. That's what you need."

So that's how it went. The husband returned, the children told him what had happened with the food, and he stayed up all night making the iron claws. Just after dawn, the Princess put them on and started her climb.

* * *

Let's pause for some comments here. We are partway through the story now. Everything in the narrative has flowed out of that first glimpse of the golden wreath. The story says that early on important things happen to us that make a tiny opening in the feeling world and a flow begins through that opening toward the Divine. Sometimes we have to remember years and years back to have a true glimpse of what made earlier openings. Antonio Machado, when he was still in the womb, was carried by his mother to a riverbank where she could see the dolphins that swam that year from the sea all the way to Seville. He remembered those dolphins. He said he saw them from inside the womb. The reality of the invisible was no problem for him. He wrote:

> I love Jesus, who said to us:
> Heaven and earth will pass away.
> When heaven and earth have passed away,
> my word will remain.
> What was your word, Jesus?
> Love? Affection? Forgiveness?
> All your words were
> one word: Wakeup!

As we read along in the tale of the White Bear, we are the youngest daughter of the King, one who loves the golden wreath and loves the being who plays with it, the Divine White Bear. We see that wreath in dreams, but where does the image of the golden wreath come from? Perhaps there have been a thousand lives, passed down, as the Tibetans might say, like the piece of wood in a relay race, from hand to hand, and never dropped. The golden wreath is one of those handovers. Finally we are the runner, and what do we do with this image we find in our hands? Well, we tell someone about it. And everyone responds to the wreath differently. Some might try to live a life utterly without sin for a year or two (ascetics and fundamentalists try that), or struggle to make works of art that resemble the golden wreath (many artists do that—I've done it for seventy years, more or less), or try to become beautiful like the wreath itself (Nijinsky tried that). But sooner or later, a voice inside us says, "The golden wreath is oval, not round. You got it wrong."

* * *

But back to the story again. When the Princess, wearing the iron claws the blacksmith had made for her, labored up the side of the Glass Mountain and arrived at the top, she was amazed to see an old-fashioned castle there, with cookhouses, dog kennels, a horse barn, and elaborate carriages. Inside the walls there was a terrace, the sort that tradespeople take over on holidays to exhibit their wares.

The Princess laid out her magic tablecloth on a big table. Soon one could smell boiled beets and the odor of squash pies. One could see shrimp in black bean sauce, roasted pheasant, watermelon pickles, and oysters on the half shell. After twenty minutes or so, the Queen of All Selfishness appeared. Long tusks grew down over her jaw. She picked a yellow songbird out of the air and ate it whole. "What have you got here, honey? You're some cook, aren't you? You don't dress worth a damn, but the setup looks good. I'm getting married three days from now, gloom-face. Can you work up a little food for the wedding?"

"This tablecloth understands a lot. If I ask it for hors d'oeuvres, I get them, cured salami if I ask for that, wedding cake if I ask for wedding cake, the real sort, made in Paris."

"What can I give you? You're here just in the nick of time. How much, honey?"

"Money doesn't work with the tablecloth. It's a gift for a gift."

"All right, what's the price? Let's hear it."

"I want one night alone with the White Bear King Valemon."

"Oh, you're something, aren't you? It won't do you any good, but if that's what you want, dear, and you're willing to pay for it, it's a go. Come inside the castle at ten o'clock tonight, and my maid will show you where the White Bear sleeps. I'll take the tablecloth now."

That's the way it happened. The deal was made. It was a good deal. But we could guess that the Divine Opera Singer of Greed has her tracks covered, and she is not worried she will lose her White Bear fiancé. And now she has the magic tablecloth as well.

Meanwhile, she went herself to the White Bear King's room, and she said to him: "The wedding is coming up. Get lots of rest. Here's a little apple wine that I made especially for you. It will help you sleep."

He drank it. It was a sleeping potion. When the Princess, full of hope, knocked later in the evening, no one answered. She walked into the room and found the Bear King sound asleep. No matter how much she talked in his ear, sang to him, and reminded him of their old days in his castle and their nights together, he showed not a trace of consciousness. He remained asleep. She waited beside him all night. At dawn she left.

She guessed that the Divine One with Tusks would come out for a stroll on the terrace. This time she brought out her magic flask, and soon she had gathered coffee cups, and teacups, and wineglasses. Using the flask, she filled them with Turkish coffee, English tea, French cognac, good vodka, expensive Riesling, and so on. When the Tusked One arrived, she was delighted.

"This is just what I need for the bridal dinner! Around here they serve you white piss and call it wine. Where'd you get all these goodies, honey?"

"My flask is a magic flask. It pours whatever you would like to have."

"Let's cut out the small talk. What do you want to get in return for this little jar?"

"I want one more night with the White Bear King Valemon."

"That must be because you had so much fun last night." Her tusks gleamed. "Give the flask to my maid at ten o'clock. She'll give you a key to his room, sweetie."

As you might expect, the Shiny-Toothed One visited the White Bear King shortly after. He was in human form, and she talked with him a bit, and poured him a good-sized drink, and waited until he drank. Then she left.

An hour or so later, the Princess—using her key—opened the door and found her lover asleep. No matter what she told him of the suffering she had gone through following his tracks, nor the old love they had had together, nor the trouble she had climbing up the glass-sided mountain, he heard not a word. Not even an eyelid fluttered. She cried until dawn came, and then she left.

The White Bear King woke in the late morning, totally ignorant of being visited. But as he left, it happened that two carpenters, who lived in the next room, were passing by. One said: "Did you realize that a woman was crying last night in your room for a long time? We heard her through the walls."

He thought to himself, "It is possible," but he said nothing.

The Princess took her place as usual on the terrace later that morning. The Queen with Double Teeth and Chin Incisors came by as usual, smelling the air. This time the Princess took out her magic shears and, shortly after, lace veils were lying on the table, and velvet skirts, a Parisian wedding gown, black traveling gloves, even a Hardanger bridal crown. The Queen of Us All came by, nibbling on a live gopher, and said, "That's perfect! I'll take the whole goddamn thing. Make sure the veil is long. What do you require? What do you want for the veil and the wedding dress?"

"One more night with the Bear King Valemon."

"You drive a hard bargain, honey. I don't know what they taught you in school. I hope you have a hot old time."

So she left. When night had come, the Gobbler of Songbirds, the Darling of All the World came to the White Bear King Valemon's room and brought him a nightcap in her usual way. He turned slightly to the side when she wasn't looking and poured the drink down his shirt into a little bag he had tied around his neck. Then after a few minutes he said, "I'm sleepy now!" and he nodded off.

Now the Horror of the Blazing Eyes, being of great intelligence, became suspicious. He seemed to be asleep, but she said to herself, "Something's not right in this room. I can smell it." She decided to test him. After a bit, she took a thick darning needle and drove it right through his upper arm. He didn't move. Not even a quiver crossed his face. "Well, I guess the handsome dog is asleep," she said. She was satisfied, and left.

This time, when the Princess entered the bedroom, the White Bear King was awake. How glad they were to see each other! They laughed and cried and told each other how terrible the waiting had been for them both. When a time of suffering is over, it seems charming to tell it all again, even if you are weeping. So they talked and talked. At dawn they heard the carpenters stirring in the next room. The Bear King thanked them for the detail they had told him, and he asked them to make a little adjustment on the wooden bridge over which the wedding party would walk. The carpenters said, "We think we can do that."

The wedding took place a few hours later. As you can imagine, it was a large production. The procession started with the bride in front, which is traditional in Norwegian weddings. The Great Mistress wore a veil over her tusks, but the winds that rushed past kept blowing it aside, and the fire coming from her eyes frightened the onlookers. The White Bear King followed behind. Many people wept. They had become fond of the Bear King and felt so sorry that he had to marry the Great One. But nothing could be done. The Queen of the Glass Mountain rules everything, and no one can say "No!" to her.

A wooden bridge led from the palace to a church on the neighboring peak.

The bridal procession walked along the path and onto the bridge. But when the Bride had just reached the midpoint, a strange thing happened. The boards gave way, for some reason, and the Queen fell with her wedding flowers down, down, hundreds of feet down. One of the carpenters had pulled a little rope, and that was that. No one should ever underestimate the power of carpenters. The sudden disappearance of the Hideous Bride was a big surprise to the onlookers. On the other hand, the wedding feast had already been laid out, the minister was ready, so why not have a wedding? So the White Bear King Valemon and his bride were married on the spot. The waiting people at the castle, and the nearby farmers and their wives, the hunters and their girlfriends, especially the carpenters and their darlings, had a great time drinking all the booze and eating the elaborate Italian dishes, chomping down the Romanian wild pheasants and Greek goat meat. After dinner they danced for hours. The wedding dance went on until all the wine and aquavit were gone; then they danced a few more hours on homemade cider and went home to their own beds.

The White Bear King and his bride in the morning started their journey back to their old house in the forest, and on the way, they stopped at the three huts and picked up, one by one, the three children! You must have guessed that the three small daughters who gave the ragged Princess the tablecloth, the magic flask, and the abundant scissors were those very children who had disappeared soon after birth. When their parents folded them back into the family, they were so glad. Their mother could now be a real mother, and their father didn't have to be a bear anymore. He could be a human person night and day.

As for me, after that great party, I woke up finally with a terrible headache, but I was happy. I saved a bottle of wine for you from the wedding party, but it fell out of my bag and broke just when I was nearly home. So here we are, whistling through our teeth as usual, with only water to drink. I don't know when we'll have another party like that!

* * *

It is said that one distinction between the genuine "teaching story" and a folktale lies in the nature of the main character. Johnny Appleseed is a human being and takes his part in an honorable folktale. The Tusked Queen of the Glass Mountain can't be contained in a tale. She is a relative of the fierce Hindu goddess Kali and belongs with the stories of excess, many of them fairy stories. The Russians like to call her Baba Yaga, or "Grandmother Yaga."

The story of the White Bear King offers us many glimpses into the divine world, which are difficult for those of us brought up in a culture that prefers not to talk seriously of spiritual excess. But the White Bear King, rolling on his back on the forest floor, tossing the wreath, and the Queen of the Glass Mountain voraciously eating everything in sight—those are some fine images of excess.

But there is a presence of God in all things, and we shouldn't be surprised then if it turns out that the Double-Toothed One is a part of God, too. After all, the golden wreath has led the King's youngest daughter directly to Her. As Western civilization goes on, we have learned to draw smaller and smaller circles representing God, and only the comforting parts of the Divine are left in. But there is a certain aspect of God that does end life. Farmers, who are breeders of cattle, pigs, and sheep, have to join with this part of God for a while at the end of each year.

The aspect of God that ends life lives on top of a glass mountain in this story, but the overeager climbers, who wear tennis shoes instead of climbing boots, fall off. The story says that you can see their bones lying all around the base of the mountain. It's very hard for people to get their minds around an Eternal Being so dangerous, she's like a nuclear power plant. Job had some sense of that, and his arguments with his three cheerful friends shed a lot of light on this matter: "Thine hands have framed me and fashioned me together round about; yet thou dost destroy me" (Job 10:8). Westerners don't want to talk about a dangerous Divinity, but the Indian people have dealt with Kali for centuries. That particular Divine Mother, when she dances, wears a necklace of human skulls to remind us of some unsavory qualities of her ecstasy.

The ability to be near danger and still feel secure comes up vividly in the early paragraphs of our Bear story. We recall that the two older daughters of the King, when riding on the White Bear's back, are asked by the Bear: "Have you ever sat more softly than you're sitting now?" They say their father's lap was softer, and they get thrown off quickly. The third girl, the youngest daughter, is asked the same question, and she says, while she is sitting on the back of a wild animal, "Never." So even with a wild animal or wild god beneath her, she can maintain that she has never felt so comfortable, nor seen so clearly, in her whole life.

Mirabai, who was a devotee of Krishna, didn't court her own safety as she worshipped Him:

> No one knows where to find the bhakti path, show me where to go.
> I would like my own body to turn into a heap of incense and
>   sandalwood and you set a torch to it.
> When I've fallen down to gray ashes, smear me on your shoulders
>   and chest.
> Mira says: You who lift the mountains, I have some light, I want
>   to mingle it with yours.

In our Norwegian story, the daughter searches everywhere through an unfamiliar landscape for the

White Bear, giving and receiving kindnesses roused by her love for Him. She will undergo deprivation, solitude, starvation, and time spent in the wilderness, where she'll gather strength of spirit and the courage necessary to be close again with the divine. In an antique version of Amor and Psyche, Apuleius's *The Golden Ass*, some of the themes are not so different from those in "The White Bear King." Apuleius shows that the heroine, Psyche, in order to fit herself for the relationship with Amor, goes through elaborate initiatory tasks, such as separating black and white seeds or gathering wool from the hazardous sheep of the golden fleece. Still, as soon as the youngest daughter has taken her place with the White Bear in his underworld castle, they simply make love. They are symbiotic, they merge, they don't need words, so they don't talk. That is lovely, and yet the lifted candle in the story implies that lovers aren't meant to live long in an unconscious way. They need some light, even if allowing light means they will have to part.

In both *The Golden Ass* and "The White Bear King Valemon" versions of the story, after the youngest daughter leaves her deliciously sensual underworld to visit her parents' home, her sisters urge her to find out more about her lover. Perhaps he has despicable habits. The two rejected and envious older daughters, still living with their parents, are eager to hear that the monster leaves hair all over the house, that his teeth are too sharp for lovemaking. They suggest that their sister get a good look at him by a good, strong light. Her mother gives her a lamp or candle and advises her to use it. The Norwegian tale adds a delicate grace note, namely, the father's advice: "I think it would be best to let things remain as they are." That advice turns out to be wrong, but it catches us for a few moments, and we can all feel our own ambiguous opinions as to whether the daughter should or should not risk the candle. The mother's advice, though, is to take the candle home with her, and some night, when the Mysterious One is asleep, lift it and see exactly who is there in her bed.

Marie-Louise von Franz, in her book *The Golden Ass of Apuleius*, and Erich Neumann, in *Amor and Psyche*, write extensively on the matter of the lifted candle, describing this desire of the soul to increase its consciousness. After time in the dark, the soul pushes for light. In human life this illumination can cause a painful break that ends a relationship for a while. The story asks what the soul is willing to pay for the increase in vision.

In the story, we have the sense that we are looking at a process that in human culture took thousands of years to transpire. We assume that in some earlier period of human life, many events—or unions—remained in the dark. We each recall memorable events in our childhood—a brother's violence, a mother's humiliation, a mysterious absence of the father, some disaster that put an uncle in prison, events that simply remained unexplained. No one spoke of those things, and if they did, there was no wit or shrewdness in the telling. Probably that darkness, that forgetfulness, the storing of frightful information somewhere else in the brain, helped early people to survive. Early people tended to live, we are told, in self-sufficient groups of forty or fifty individuals. Strangers might come and kill ten or fifteen of the clan. Some scientists believe these events are stored in the memory in such a way as to avoid serious disruptions. Brain researchers say that the amygdala sends these memories to the hypothalamus for storage. Once there, the memory is difficult to access. This "forgetting" or "storing" would allow the tribe to continue with their essential tasks for survival.

How do we know that many religious and ecstatic experiences in our youth similarly dropped down into forgetfulness? Possibly fairy tales themselves are ways to keep the early joys of our life concealed and yet not lost. To write poetry means to lift Psyche's candle, as Emily Dickinson did. She wrote:

> Exultation is the going
> Of an inland soul to sea,
> Past the houses—past the headlands—
> Into deep Eternity—
>
> Bred as we, among the mountains,
> Can the sailor understand
> The divine intoxication
> Of the first league out from land?

Did we want the candle to be lifted above our experiences? In a relationship dominated by the moon, by night, by the deep delights of night-joys, we would rather not be disturbed. But if we don't lift the candle, we never know more than the one inchoate part of the one we love.

In this story, the Princess watches in horror as the Bear rushes out of his own palace and plunges madly into the forest. She clings desperately to his fur, but the branches and sharp twigs in the forest finally pull her away. A girl who has been living with a divine being must return to the normal, boring, bitter, limited, and sad human state. Scratched up and wandering, she will move through years of spiritual poverty and loneliness. Perhaps this stage will take up twenty years in the middle of her life. These days, busy in a career, a man or woman feels left to wander alone in the forest, with no food and no companionship. As the Persian poet Hafez wrote: "The light in the hermit's hut goes out in the earthly church."

Those of us reading those words know that we, too, have been walking along, getting scratched up in the woods, the light gone out of us, unable to imagine an end to the wandering. University degrees don't really help with this problem. We have to experience the desperation that comes with not being fed before we can enter the next part of the story. César Vallejo said:

> And what if after so much history, we succumb,
> not to eternity,
> but to these simple things, like being
> at home, or starting to brood!
> What if we discover later
> all of a sudden, that we are living
> to judge by the height of the stars
> off a comb and off stains on a handkerchief!
> It would be better, really,
> if it were all swallowed up, right now!

We mustn't assume from the jokey tone tellers of fairy tales use that there is little at stake here. Everything is at stake.

In the myth, the Bear King and the Awesome Lady of Vast Appetite, whom he almost marries, belong to a wild side of the universe. Greek tales around Dionysus spoke of a wildness beyond human beings that is capable of tearing and destroying them. Possibly in some pre-industrial, pre-agricultural time, women and men may have been able to sustain a longer union with the wild energies of deities. But with a civilizing emphasis on intellect and light, we are separated from the Awesome Lady and the Bear King, who represent our instincts, as well as our ability to experience both the animal and the divine.

Turning to the story again, once the soul agrees to give the true self to the Divine (Saint John of the Cross did that as well), then we get to the Bear King's castle, where the Divine lives. But what if it turns out that we can meet the Divine only at night? Everything is dark at night. We might be aware of a few moments of the ecstatic, but that's all we know. What we do know for sure is that something happened with humans, something after Creation but before Egypt. The expulsion from the Garden, which the northern European artists in Dürer's time painted so passionately, so broken-heartedly, so grievingly, probably touches that moment of lifting the candle, which seems to be one of the most important things that ever happened to human beings. One could say that before the lifting, we had Union; but after it, Union and Separation both. Hafez says:

Both union with you and separation from you
Confuse me. What can I do? You are not present
Nor are you utterly absent from my sight.

In another poem he says:

How blessed is the man who, like Hafez,
Has tasted in his heart the wine made before Adam.

So the wine made before Adam is the wine that is drunk in the castle when all is dark. Even though we are exiled from the castle, tramping alone through the woods, we are not exiled permanently. We move back and forth between Union and Separation. Hafez adds:

Your perch is on the lote tree in Paradise,
Oh wide-seeing hawk. What are you doing
Crouching in this mop-closet of calamity?

When we are in separation, we keep asking people if they have seen the Divine Bear go by; they always say they saw him last week, so the Divine is not far ahead. But the informants also warn that there's grave danger of a lasting separation. "He's about to be married!" When we are in separation, it is important to teach small children, feed the starving family of the blacksmith, to have metal claws in addition to dancing slippers; it is important to have something to trade, and start trading, and not be freaked out by the gross and enormous Greedy Soul—even if it is our own. Even in separation, we can recall the generosity of Union, its ecstatic energy. The magic tablecloth, flask, and scissors help us remember. They are reminders of the joy of Union.

Have we come now to the hut at the base of the Glass Mountain? The blacksmith's children live there. They, unlike the three happy children she played with earlier, are starving. "Sometimes our mother puts stones in the boiling water and tells us they are apples, and it really does help." These are the starving children inside us, and feeding them is like reading the poems of Keats, or adding brilliant colors to the painting we've begun of the apple orchard, or practicing a musical instrument for hours every day. While we do this, the blacksmith gives us iron claws that are like form in art, like discipline in spiritual life, like memorizations of holy texts.

With the iron claws, we can engage teachers or artists who seemed too difficult to us before. Rilke gets fingers and metal so close together in these lines:

when the wrestlers' sinews
grew long like metal strings,
he felt them under his fingers
like chords of deep music.

With the help of iron, the soul eventually gets to the top of the Glass Mountain. To her amazement, a castle has been built up there. She knows she will soon meet the Master of Appetite, the Greedy Soul itself. Muslims are familiar with the *nafs*, their name for the Greedy Soul. The Muslim visualization of that force includes the dragon. Rumi says:

The *nafs* is the mother of idols! A common idol
is a snake; this one is a dragon.

Abu Bakr, the early Sufi teacher, says of human greed-iness,

It is like fire: When at the point of being extinguished, it always flares up somewhere else. If the *nafs* is calmed in one area, it ignites in another.

Some say that infidelity is doing what the *nafs* wants. . . . In our story, it appears as the Lady of the Glass Mountain. The *nafs* is the Master of Demands, the King of Desires, the Queen of Unreasonable Insistence. Whoever knows his own *nafs* knows his god.

Our story offers some brilliant depictions of the *nafs*. The Queen of the Glass Mountain comes up to the table on which the Princess has spread the magic tablecloth; this table is now weighed down with roasted chicken, oysters in the half shell, gefilte fish, baby pigs, goose liver, Greek olives, lamb joints, and so on. She gobbles down a dozen roasted larks, feathers and all, and then mentions that she will need a wedding spread three days hence. She wants to know what she'll have to pay for the magic cloth. "One night with the White Bear King" is the deal, but we are a little suspicious that the deal won't go through. The *nafs* is famous for drugging human beings just before they come into the presence of the one they love. The Queen of the

Glass Mountain does just that to the White Bear King, so he is asleep when the Princess arrives at his room. She tries all night to wake him; she shakes him; nothing works, and then the night is over.

The next morning, when she sets out the magic flask, capable of providing whatever liquid anyone could want, the fragrance of its contents attracts the wandering Monster of Greed, so a deal is made a second time—the magic flask for one more night with the White Bear King. This repeats, as we know, with much bargaining, frustration, and weeping, until carpenters from next door whisper to the King that they have heard a woman weeping, and he finally understands that his dear wife has come. He kept that welcome information in his heart all day and determined that the conversation with the Big-Toothed Queen would go differently that night.

We could say that the Princess who befriends the White Bear stands for each one of us. Each one of us feels lucky at the start, experiences a memory of the golden wreath, is chosen as a bride, goes to the White Bear's palace, and knows the mysterious Love at Night. Experiencing the Bear's love at night is like seeing poems written in one's own handwriting that one cannot remember writing, poems that seem to take part in all the sweetness of the Divine.

Of course, our parents have many questions about our lover, and our ugly sisters are jealous, and soon all the ecstasy of early adolescence is gone and we are stumbling through the woods, ragged, deserted, and lost, like everyone else. That state can last for years, as we all know. It can be an unfortunate "marriage," a "career," an obsession.

All during the ecstatic time, and the stumbling abandonment, though we don't know it, we are headed for the Glass Mountain. That is, we are headed toward a confrontation with the Greedy One, who wasn't even mentioned until most of the action of the story has already happened. So where did She come from? Well, we can only proceed through our life by paying close attention to the psychic field of that *nafs*-ness, and by feeding it judiciously and tenderly out there on the terrace. Knowing about the Greedy One, as we know it by studying literature, will not be enough. She has to be attended to where she lives, inside each of us. Her appetite grows more ferocious as she senses the shift to a more conscious attitude, since that will mean a diminishment of her power. You recognize her appetite and you feed her something. You can't fill her enormous greediness, which is always eating, eating, eating as tigers eat deer, as whales eat plankton, as sharks eat sailors. She is in the last month of Ahab's life, when nothing is left of life but the sharpened harpoons, the massive teeth of Moby Dick, and the whirling, insane greediness of the one-legged Puritan madman determined to be present at the wedding of death and eternity.

And while this is going on, your task and your delight is to fill your own cup with sweetness, "before it fills with dust." In the poem "Stealing Sugar from the Castle" I have tried to say how that goes in my life.

STEALING SUGAR FROM THE CASTLE

We are poor students who stay after school to study joy.
We are like those birds in the India mountains.
I am a widow whose child is her only joy.

The only thing I hold in my ant-like head
Is the builder's pan of the castle of sugar.
Just to steal one grain of sugar is a joy!

Like a bird, we fly out of darkness into the hall,
Which is lit with singing, then fly out again,
Being shut out of the warm hall is also a joy.

I am a laggard, a loafer, and an idiot. But I love
To read about those who caught one glimpse
Of the Face, and died twenty years later in joy.

I don't mind your saying I will die soon.
Even in the sound of the word soon, *I hear*
The word you *which begins every sentence of joy.*

"You're a thief!" the judge said. "Let's see
Your hands!" I showed my calloused hands in court.
My sentence was a thousand years of joy.

ACKNOWLEDGMENTS

With deepest gratitude to the master storyteller Gioia Timpanelli, a rare being who has followed the wisdom of fairy stories all her days.

Many thanks to Libby Burton, an enthusiastic supporter of this project since she first saw it. Her welcoming of the material and her fine and careful editing have been a great blessing.

At times in the last twenty years, people have read portions of this book and given me valuable advice; I am thankful to each of them.

ABOUT THE AUTHOR

ROBERT BLY is the author of numerous books of poetry, including *The Light Around the Body*, winner of the National Book Award, and, most recently, *Talking into the Ear of a Donkey*. He is also the author of many works of nonfiction, including *Iron John: A Book About Men*, which was an international bestseller and a pioneering work in the men's movement. His awards include the Poetry Society of America's Frost Medal for distinguished lifetime achievement in poetry. He lives in Minneapolis.